LAUREL'S DIARY

A Memoir of Trauma, Intimacy, and the Work of Reclamation

GINA DIMARCO

Published by Stillwater Press

Stillwater Press publishes rigorously edited narrative nonfiction examining psychological injury, recovery, and moral complexity through lived experience.

First edition

ISBN: 979-8-9858390-9-8
Library of Congress Control Number: 2026902967
Cover design by Lisa Barker Design
Interior design by Muhammad Bilal
Printed in the United States of America

For the women who negotiated their way back to themselves —
and for those who have only just begun.

Table of Contents

CONTENT NOTE

i

This memoir contains descriptions of sexual assault and its aftermath. It also includes references to intimacy and trauma that may be difficult for some readers.

AUTHOR'S NOTE

This book does not reconstruct trauma from a safe distance. It preserves it as it unfolded—unevenly, imperfectly, and without the benefit of hindsight. Some passages appear as emails, texts, or diary entries written in the moment; others step briefly into third person. That distance is intentional. In the aftermath of violence, I often experienced myself as both participant and observer, present and removed. The shifting forms in these pages reflect that fracture. I have resisted smoothing the narrative into coherence, not out of carelessness, but because coherence was not available to me then. What follows is not a completed arc, but a record of learning once again to trust the process of healing, intimate relationships, and above all, myself.

PROLOGUE

———✕———

Around 10 p.m. on a random Monday in February, Laurel was folding laundry while texting her boyfriend, Chris. She had just folded a pair of pants when she heard a knock at her door.

Who on earth could that possibly be? she thought as she made her way to answer it. Dressed only in her robe and nightgown, she wasn't interested in company. She peeked through the window and saw a face she hadn't seen in almost a year—Seth.

They had gone on two dates, both monumental failures. The first was a blind date organized by an old colleague of Laurel's, Krista.

"You're gonna love him, Laurel," she had said. "He's totally your type."

The date was a disaster, with Seth focusing the conversation solely on himself and how successful he was. Laurel politely declined any future dates.

About a year later, after Krista insisted that his behavior the first night had been a result of nerves, Laurel agreed to a second date—not because she was interested, but because she hoped it would appease her friend.

If it still goes down in flames, at least she can't say I didn't try, Laurel had thought.

The second date was even worse than the first. They met at a restaurant where he was so grotesquely rude to the waitress that Laurel left before the appetizers arrived. She paid an estimated portion of the bill and—in front of Seth—left the waitress a large tip, apologizing for his horrific behavior. Seth was angry, but Laurel didn't care. He followed her to her car, but she ignored him, got in, and drove home.

In the weeks afterward, she was inundated with countless emails and text messages not only from Seth, but Krista as well. Seth vacillated between anger and insincere apologies, while Krista made excuses and opined that Laurel had simply misread his humor. Eventually, Laurel blocked them both across all communication channels.

So why, then, was he standing on her doorstep at 10 p.m. on a random Monday in February?

She knew he had friends in the area and, given the way he swayed on the porch, surmised he was drunk. She cracked the door open slightly, intending to ask whether he needed help getting an Uber.

Maybe he's just lost, she thought. *Or his car broke down and he remembered I was nearby.*

As soon as she opened the door, his blurry eyes locked onto hers. Before she could ask what, he wanted, he pushed against the door. Laurel immediately realized her mistake and tried desperately to force it closed. Her children were sleeping upstairs, and she was suddenly terrified of this man being in the house with them.

Seth was an active Air Force reservist and much stronger than Laurel. He forced his way through the door, so Laurel planted herself at the foot of the stairs. For a moment, Seth looked confused, unsure of what to do; it was as though he hadn't thought he would get this far. Then he glanced at Laurel in her robe, and primal instinct overtook him.

Knowing she could not stop what was about to happen, Laurel did the only thing she could think to do: she quietly turned on her phone's camera and pressed record. She then vowed to keep things as quiet as possible so as not to wake her children. The thought of them coming downstairs to see what was happening terrified her more than the violence she understood was about to come.

The assault lasted ten minutes. In those ten minutes, she was left bruised and bleeding—but alive.

He walked out of the house—the door still ajar from when he had forced his way in—as though he had simply forgotten his keys. Laurel crawled to the door, closed it, and locked it. Then she made her way upstairs to check on her still-sleeping children.

Thank God, she thought. *Thank Gosd.*

Recognizing the importance of preserving evidence to use against him, she prepared herself for the hospital. She called three people before one responded. That friend, Michel, quickly came over to watch her children while she went to the ER. Not realizing what had happened—but knowing it was serious enough to warrant support—Michel called his wife, Sunny, who met Laurel at the hospital after she had been triaged but before she was examined by the sexual assault team.

Over the next few months, Laurel kept things to herself. She struggled to process her trauma. Her default method was compartmentalization. Her goal was survival, and survival meant pretending during the day that she wasn't a broken, bleeding mess.

But the compartmentalization began to take its toll, and she turned to writing.

Since middle school, she had kept a diary in which she wrote to herself—the deepest part of herself—to sort through problems, fears, and moments of joy. She laid herself bare on those pages, finding a clarity she could not reach through spoken words.

Writing was her outlet, her therapy, her salvation.

The man who would become her husband understood this and dove headfirst into her unruly sea of words. Together, they would carry Laurel back to herself.

FIRST CONTACT

Laurel told Chris about the assault a few days after it happened. She struggled to have that conversation but was strongly encouraged by the friends who had helped her in its aftermath.

She called him but did not go into detail—only offering a brief explanation that it had happened, that she had been examined and cataloged by the hospital, and that Michel and Sunny were helping. Because she and Chris were in a long-distance relationship, it was the best she could manage.

In the days that followed, they texted only briefly—a far cry from their usual playful banter. Laurel was busy navigating the legal, medical, and emotional ramifications, while Chris was trapped half a country away. He wanted to come to her, but Laurel begged him not to. She didn't want him to see the bruises and pain—still terribly raw—on her face. He complied only because he understood her need to retain some semblance of control.

This was the first real message he had sent that explicitly acknowledged what had transpired. It was his first attempt to bridge the divide, knowing she was not yet capable of doing so herself.

***

To: Laurel

From: Chris

I imagine you're having a rough go of things. I wish I could be there to do something—anything—for you. If you need me, just say the word. Know that I do love you, and I haven't stopped thinking of or worrying about you, but I'm giving you the space to handle things how you see fit. Call me any time, for any reason, even if it's just to talk shop. I love you.

— — — — —

To: Chris

From: Laurel

I really needed to read that.

Truth is, while I'm obviously upset that this happened for a multitude of reasons, I'm most upset about the potential (or even realized) impact it will have—or is having—on us.

I don't want to pretend there won't be negative fallout from this. Just... please be honest and open with me as it manifests. I won't take offense, and I won't hold anything against you. I just need you to be honest with me about how you feel.

As for me, I'm physically better than where I started. The bruises are fading, and I'm able to breathe without pain. The migraine comes and goes, but that tends to reflect crying more than anything else. I'm sleeping in spurts (which is better than not at all), and while I'm not starving (I promise I'm not), I know I've got to do better about eating.

Emotionally, I'm disappointed in myself for a thousand different reasons. And while I know logically I wasn't at fault, none of this would've happened had I told him to pound sand rather than open the door. I'm vehemently angry that this happened with the boys upstairs, but at the same time, I'm incredibly grateful nothing resulted from them being there. If anything, it subdued me enough that I didn't end up getting myself killed.

I'm mostly scared of what this means for us. I'm trying to be super pragmatic, so I wouldn't take anything as a slight against me (because I know your intention would never be to hurt me), but that tendency of mine to play scenario association? It's not fun. And none of those scenarios end well, given what's at stake. That kills me more than anything else.

I'm not suicidal, but the thought did cross my mind to light the bed on fire and burn everything away with it—myself included. It was a moment of sheer desperation as I struggled to come to terms with being in a body that no longer feels like mine.

I don't want me. I don't want this. I spent all of yesterday trying to pretend I didn't exist. I forced myself to go to work today, hating myself and everyone around me for their pity and the "It's not your fault" bullshit #MeToo has taught us all to say.

I hate that he's likely going to walk. Did you know only 3 percent of assault survivors see any sort of justice? And even with my video, thanks to things like *Fifty Shades of Grey*, a lawyer can make it sound as if I were role-playing. The advocate was supposed to call me back but still hasn't. A nurse from the hospital did, though, to check on me, which I thought was really kind. They've got an incredible program there—things that never would've occurred to me but helped so much that night.

They keep a closet of brand-new underwear and bras on hand to replace the ones taken for evidence. They also have a special camera and a small, flexible ruler used to catalog wounds and bruising for the kit. And did you know they even have specialized nurses on call 24/7 who are specifically trained to collect DNA evidence? I wonder if all hospitals have programs like that. Anyway, the nurse said the advocate should be calling me and seemed surprised that I hadn't already heard from her. It's so frustrating because I have no idea what I'm supposed to do next, and she, supposedly, helps me sort it out.

Logically, I've pulled myself together. Emotionally, I'm just not there. And I don't know how to get there. I just trust that, eventually, I will.

— — — — —

To: Laurel

From: Chris

This is really challenging to respond to, because I don't know how it's affected us. I don't know how deep the scars are going to go. I don't know if you'll get justice. I don't know if you'll be able to look at me the same way you did before. I don't know how you'll approach romance and sex anymore. It's all up in the air. I've never been with someone who was violently raped while I was 1,200 miles away. In more than just a manner of speaking, we're both in a dark cave, bouncing off its walls. As for honesty, I don't know that it does either of us any good to act otherwise.

I'm glad your body is healing. I'm really glad you are mindful of your health and not wasting away. I know you already know this, but those boys need you in top shape, no matter what pain you're going through.

Something I do need from you (when you're ready) is clarity on who this guy was and how this started. My head was spinning when we talked on the phone. You were crying, and it was hard to piece any of it together. I suspect he was larger and stronger than you, and that you were being your characteristically thoughtful self. The fact that he knew there were boys in the house makes this all the worse. If one of them had heard a commotion and come down to investigate, it would have scarred him for life (or, heaven forbid, the asshole hurt him as well). At the very least, we can be thankful that didn't happen. But again, the cost can't be their mother. They need you. All of you.

If I'm honest, I know that in the vast majority of cases, long-distance relationships don't work.

If I'm honest, rape victims tend to have long-term trust issues and problems bonding with the opposite sex.

...but if I'm also honest, it doesn't matter. Statistics are for trends, not individuals. I know you're a surprising and amazing woman, and this doesn't change how I feel about you. But that isn't really what matters. What matters is how you respond to this. If you go down the hole, I can't follow you. There are things I want to do. There's a family I want to build. And that doesn't leave a lot of room for someone stuck in a traumatic event. I need a first mate, not a boat anchor.

The betting man in me says you're the first mate. And if there's anything I can do at all to help ensure that, you have to tell me. I'm too far away, and I'm just guessing from out here. I want to support you however I can.

I will say, too, that if you need to take your time coming back, and can't bear the weight of a relationship, I understand. This whole show is about what's right for you and your boys, and I'm the smallest part of that equation at the moment. As your friend, your lover, your love, I want only what is best for you, and I'll be okay if you decide that a ticket to Splitsville is what you need.

That's not to say it won't be utterly devastating, or that I won't be completely heartbroken—because I will be. But I'll live.

I'm sorry the advocate hasn't reached back out yet, but I'm glad the hospital has things in place to give you your best shot at justice. DNA collection and small comforts in the midst of chaos are steps in the right direction.

As for placations, you know that's not my style. I'm the muscle. My "placations" are simply wrapping you up in my arms and resting your head on my chest. It'll take time and intention, like anything else. You'll heal, and we'll move on from this. But I caution you to reach out to someone experienced in trauma who can help you. I can only do so much. Sunny and Michel can only do so much. Together, we'll get through this. I love you.

VERBAL VOMIT

In promising to reach out for help beyond Chris, Sunny and Michel, Laurel knew that her best prospect for trauma-informed assistance would be through Kiera, a friend of hers in New York who had received assault response training due to her previous job as a Residential Aid for her university. Thus, upon collecting herself after reading Chris' e-mail, she drafted another destined for New York.

***

To: Kiera

From: Laurel

I'm a certifiable mess. However, I'm physically okay and even relatively okay emotionally (although it won't sound like it). I just need to work through some stuff with someone who can't physically interact with me, who I won't visually see, and who I don't have to hear (no offense, okay? I mean absolutely no offense by that). I need communication wholly void of that stuff.

On Monday night, with the boys asleep in their beds upstairs, I was raped by an acquaintance.

He was inebriated, so I thought he needed help calling Uber or something. He came in and was talking loudly enough that I was concerned the boys would wake up, so

I planted myself firmly between him and the staircase, asking him to quiet down. My bedroom is right next to the front door, and I was wearing a nursing gown (A NURSING GOWN) and robe, so it's not like I was wearing anything sexy. I know I don't have to explain it to you, but I still feel compelled to explain it anyway.

Things quickly went south, and what happened, happened. The boys didn't wake up and when all was said and done, he basically walked out the front door (which was still open) as though nothing happened. He didn't run out like he was trying to get away from the cops; he seriously just moseyed out of the damned house as though he'd forgotten his keys, came back in to get them, and waltzed back out again.

The entire thing happened over the course of about ten minutes. Probably not even a full ten minutes.

When I realized there was no escaping the assault, I turned my phone's camera on in an attempt to videotape evidence to nail this bastard. I'm not completely stupid. I know all the stats about these dickheads walking free because he said/she said never works in our favor. I was NOT about to let anyone claim this was in ANY WAY consensual.

Sunny stayed with me at the hospital all throughout the evidence collection/exam. We were there until after 5AM. I'm eternally grateful to have had her there. And Michel, too. I didn't tell Chris anything. Didn't mention anything to anyone because how do you do that (I mean hell... this e-mail is just going swimmingly, right?).

I took two days off from work because I couldn't function. I went back to work yesterday, which was probably a mistake, but I'm trying really hard to inject some "normal" back into things. Make myself feel human again.

Michel and Sunny kept telling me I needed to tell Chris, and while I knew they were right, I was pretty damned set against it. I finally told him, though, and as expected, it's been fuck-all since. And that's not his fault. There's no guidebook for this crap. I'm honestly not angry with him. I'm upset, I'm scared, and I'm railing against every-thing/everyone.

This whole situation has me feeling like a tiny marble being smashed around a pinball machine. I'm constantly being hurled up, falling down, thrown left and then slammed right. I can't get a hold on anything.

And I know this is all normal. I know that it doesn't all get processed at once, and even if you feel like you're good, you're probably gonna lose your shit at some point when you realize there's more to process. I know none of this is my fault (I swear if I hear that again from someone, I'm gonna scream), but I don't 100% believe it, because if I had just NOT opened the door, this never would've happened.

And then there's Chris. The boys are safe. I'm technically safe. Things could have been so much worse, but they weren't. Yay, right? And I'm grateful for that. I swear I'm grateful for that. But now I feel like things that were going SO WELL for Chris and I... it's all ruined. I feel ruined.

I'm angry with myself because I'm the one who champions logic over feeling. I know this is something you and I differ on, but feelings are terrible indicators of reality, so feelings should be secondary to fact. If feelings aren't matching with facts, the problem is not in the facts but with the feelings, and the feelings need to be addressed.

I don't know how to address my feelings to get them in-line with reality because they are so strong. Every. single. thing. inside me is screaming that I'm damaged.

I legitimately want to light my bed on fire and sit in the middle as it burns because I feel so uncomfortable in my own skin. I'm not suicidal, mind you. I recognize that the intense disdain I have for my body will lessen as time goes on and I come to (better) terms with things, and I wouldn't hurt myself because I have kids who need me. I'm sharing that to highlight the intensity of my feelings. My shitty, shitty, environmentally jacked up feelings that have zero basis in reality and have been born of trauma and raised in fear.

I. Hate. This.

But yes. Chris. I told him, and I hate that I told him. If I could, I'd take it back. I'd take it back and never tell him because at least then I wouldn't feel this guilt for not only making him feel like he'd failed in some manner, but guilt for ruining us.

Chris wants kids. You don't want kids with someone who might have an STD. He wants someone smart and capable — not an idiot who legitimately lets an asshole into the house while the kids are sleeping upstairs. He wants someone emotionally stable and mature, and I feel like I've been catapulted back to my tweens. And I don't know if this is a self-fulfilling prophecy or what, but it's almost like I'd rather just cut ties with him now so it doesn't get dragged out as he arrives at the same conclusion: this is not worth the trouble.

Mind you, I recognize that Chris is not the type of man to do this. I know Chris is a good man, which is probably why I want to cut and run, because it would be so much easier for me to handle that than for him to recognize my inherent brokenness. The idea of him looking at me as though I'm now less... I'd take burning on the bed over that.

My God, I need to stop. I've written War and Peace over here. It's like I'm desperately trying to build a complete account—maybe if I say everything, nothing worse can happen.

So why am I sending this to you? Because you're up in New York and can't try hugging me or holding my hand. And if you call (please don't), I can (and will) ignore you (sorry, sorry, sorry) because I simply can't handle hearing "It's not your fault" or undertones of sadness/pity. I can't. I'm so beyond done with all of it. So please, please, please don't think I don't value you or want your friendship.

On the contrary... I do! I'm reaching out to you because I know I need better help and I want it from someone who is busy enough that she won't feel the need to constantly check in and can ONLY check in non-physically. Does that make sense? So again, please don't take offense to any of the ramblings. I value you so much and know you're probably the best resource I have in addition to Sunny.

And while I know you're married to Steve and you share everything (as you should), when you share this with him, do me a favor and tell him that he is to go ahead and pretend he knows nothing. I want no acknowledgement from him whatsoever that he's sorry this happened or that he's there if I should need him. And you know I love Steve. I love him ridiculous amounts and appreciate him and none of this makes me appreciate or love him less. I just can't handle the idea of being treated differently. I know he wouldn't treat me as less, but I don't want to be treated with extra gentleness or any of that crap. I just want normalcy. I want to pretend none of this happened and ignore all fallout. But I can't. I know that. So here I am.

BTW, I'm not looking for a response right away. I just needed to get this all out. You're probably going to want to call, but I'm going to ignore you if you do. I feel like a TOTAL ASSHOLE for admitting that, but at least I'm an honest asshole.

— — — — —

Kiera: I'm not planning to tell Steve for the foreseeable future. He's actually sending you an invite to come up for a visit, and that's all on his own. I'm totally comfortable keeping this private.

Laurel: I'm honestly fine with you telling him; I just don't want to know about it. I never want to be a source of secrets between a husband and wife.

Kiera: I don't see it as a secret. If it's more helpful for people not to know, then it's for the best. This way, you don't have to guess.

Laurel: Okay. Chris and I did talk last night. He and I are up in the air; it sucks, but it's reality.

Kiera: Up in the air because of this or before this?

Laurel: Because of this.

Kiera: Can you explain why?

I'm trying to be supportive—but from an outside perspective, I'm struggling to see how an asshole attacking you should or would interfere with your relationship.

Laurel: It's a "how do we go on from here, given all the shit that this situation causes long term" sort of thing.

Kiera: I'm trying to approach this logically because you said you wanted less consoling and more logic, but if I need to readjust, I'd be happy to.

Laurel: I definitely appreciate the logic. After the email from Chris and the subsequent conversation, I realized I might've overdone my stress on logic and truth with him. In my defense, I didn't realize that my request was a terrible one. In his, neither did he.

So, while honesty and logic are what I need from you, for example, what I need from him is less brutal honesty and more optimistic support. I'm not wanting him to lie or create a false image of reality, but maybe not point

out the various ways this has or could
impact us.

He wasn't mean or even negative in his
response to me. For as much as it may
have hurt reading it, I recognize his
intention was only to do as I had asked.
He's trying really hard to just do so
because he understands my need to feel
in control again. None of what he said
surprised me. He vocalized all the
various fears I had regarding the
potential impact this will have on us.

I appreciated his honesty, but upon
reading it and feeling the impact of it
coming from him, there's no denying
how hurtful it was. I don't blame him for
that; he simply did as I asked. He was
pragmatic and honest. I just know better
than to ask for that again right now—at
least from him. I thought I was able to
handle it; I was not.

Kiera: I'm so sorry to hear that. Do you
think there's room to ask for a
readjustment of his approach?

Laurel: Maybe, but right now it's radio
silence unless I send a message. He's just
trying to give me the space I asked for.

FIRST MEETUP

Up to this point, Laurel's life had been full. She was advancing in a career she loved, managing days that moved quickly. At home, she moved between a burgeoning toddler and a special-needs child, helping them navigate their respective worlds. Chris—once just a friend—had become something more, easily and without warning. She was tired, sure, but capable and accustomed to meeting whatever each day required. A weekend away was a rare luxury.

Laurel and Chris had been looking forward to their Florida weekend for months. After the assault, Laurel wasn't sure she wanted to go on the trip at all, let alone face Chris so soon. She still had a couple of stitches on her back that hadn't fully healed, and the idea of being physically intimate with him felt overwhelming. Still, Chris was adamant that they keep their plans, and Laurel didn't want to disappoint him.

Laurel arrived first and tried mentally to prepare herself for Chris' arrival. Her heart thumped so loudly in her chest that she was certain the car rental agent could hear it. Breathing felt impossible at times, and the humid Florida air clung to her lungs, making her feel smothered. Chris arrived a few hours later, and her heart rate escalated as she waited for him to walk through the door. The moment she saw him, her soul leapt. She may have been afraid of the uncertainty, but her love for him far outpaced her fear.

In that moment, Laurel recognized how wrong she had been to push him away for so long. Had she let him come home when everything first happened, it might have spared them both some pain.

The drive from the airport to the hotel was brief, and it was late by the time they entered the lobby. They stepped into the elevator, and for the first time since the assault, Chris wrapped Laurel in his arms. She allowed it tentatively, still unsure how to feel inside her own body. His shirt felt smooth against her face, and he smelled fresh—somehow untouched by the heat.

Soon they were in the hotel room. Laurel had decided that sex needed to happen sooner rather than later. In her mind, it was the elephant in the room: *Can she be intimate with Chris after everything that happened?* She was determined to win that battle.

Chris had said from the outset that he would follow her lead. This had to originate with her; he didn't want to make an already difficult thing harder. She settled into bed against him. He kissed her softly, again and again. To Laurel, it almost felt as though he were trying gently to kiss away the memory of what had happened. She was impatient to move past this hurdle. She focused on the mechanics—touch, breath, proximity—naively trusting that if she could get through this, she would be healed.

So Laurel moved her hands over his body. She tried not to flinch as he moved his hands over hers in return. When she became overwhelmed, she centered herself against his chest. Resting her head there, she could hear his heartbeat and feel the warmth that inevitably felt like home. He held her until she was ready, and soon they found their rhythm.

They didn't speak much that night. Instead, they allowed themselves to rest in the quiet victory of that first intimacy and fell asleep in each other's arms, daring to hope that maybe—just maybe—tomorrow wouldn't feel as Sisyphean as it once had.

EARLY SETBACKS AND SUCCESS

——— ✕ ———

The next morning, emboldened by the fragile success of the night before, they once again found themselves a tangled mess of limbs. Chris took a chance and pushed Laurel slightly further than he had the night before. Like her, he was trying to navigate the path forward by locating the guardrails. He suggested moving into a position that set off more than a few alarm bells for Laurel. She tensed and admitted she wasn't ready. He accepted that and made a mental note to tread carefully around positions that might be triggering for her.

Later, Chris asked about the assault. Laurel tried to answer honestly, but she has a tendency to grow quiet while thinking through difficult responses, and her extended silences began to stir frustration and anxiety in Chris, who felt as though she might be hiding something.

He had only ever known her to be forthcoming and open throughout their many years of friendship. This version of her unsettled him. He pressed—probably too hard in the moment. She shut down, unsure how to proceed because every possible answer felt destructive. Chris stepped out, believing that distance and breathing room might give them both a chance to recalibrate.

Unfortunately, the distance that felt constructive to Chris was devastating to Laurel. Where he saw space, she saw abandonment. As she struggled to navigate her feelings—searching for words that would be meaningful but not overwhelming—she experienced his departure as confirmation that she was too much.

She felt doubly discarded and hopelessly broken. If even Chris couldn't bear to stay, how could anyone else? Worse, she began to fear that he no longer believed her—that he thought she had somehow participated in what happened. That suspicion fractured her in ways she struggled to articulate.

She contemplated giving him the audio recording. Maybe that would make him understand. But she could barely endure the memory herself and couldn't bring herself to pass the nightmare on to him. She felt trapped between her need to prove herself and her instinct to protect him. She wept silently, her emotions robbing her of speech.

After some time apart, Chris realized he might have pushed too hard. He recognized his own baggage—lingering suspicion shaped by past experiences of manipulation—but couldn't reconcile that baggage with the woman he knew Laurel to be. That realization sent him back to her. He pulled her close and apologized.

Laurel's tears continued, but her frozen body gradually softened in his arms.

"If this is too much, we don't have to continue," he repeated. "You tell me what you need to tell me when you're ready."

Slowly, Laurel found her voice again and answered the questions that had been plaguing him. Chris' anxiety eased. He was learning that if he wanted to support Laurel well, he would need to set aside his own fear and frustration. He believed he was capable of that work, and he believed Laurel was worth it. He began to trust that he could help guide them both through the storm.

At dinner that evening, they talked about how good it felt to have weathered that moment together. They confessed their anxieties going into the trip—particularly around intimacy and the possibility of triggering setbacks. They felt stronger as a couple and, perhaps a little naively, believed the worst was behind them.

THE NIGHTMARE

——— ✕ ———

That night, Laurel had a nightmare, and her body responded viscerally. Her movements woke Chris, who in turn tried to jostle her out of the dream. It was the first time Laurel became aware of the subconscious effects of the assault.

When Chris woke her, she was disoriented and confused. Her heart raced, and she was sweating as though she had just finished running a marathon. The bedsheets were drenched, and she felt nauseated. For a moment, she couldn't reconcile how she was in bed with Chris when, only seconds earlier, she had been fighting off Seth.

Chris carefully pulled her into his arms and kissed her head, saying, "You were having a bad dream. You're safe. I'm here."

She then noticed she was shivering. Her entire body trembled, and she couldn't figure out why. Chris noted that it was probably adrenaline coursing through her; that would explain the sweating and racing heartbeat. He asked whether she had these nightmares often, and for a moment, she couldn't answer.

As her mind emerged from the fog of sleep into reality, all she could focus on was the intense shame and guilt she felt for still being so irreparably broken.

After all, she had spent the entire weekend trying to prove how "okay" she was. Now he was quite literally holding her together as she fell apart in his arms. The façade of "okay" had evaporated.

"I'm fine, I'm fine," she said, pushing him away. "I'm sorry I woke you up. I'm just going to get some air."

She went into the living room and opened her computer, attempting to redirect her mind away from spiraling. Chris, unsure how far to push, let her go.

Unfortunately, even as Laurel fired off a few work emails, she couldn't ignore the truth: what she thought she had under control was decidedly not under control.

It was then that she decided to return to her diary.

STITCHES

———— ✕ ————

The next morning, as Laurel stood before the mirror finishing her makeup, Chris stepped behind her and pulled her into an embrace. She winced, and he immediately stepped back, afraid he had triggered her. She saw the guilt flash across his face and shook her head.

"No, no—you just touched my stitches."

Confusion, then anger, raged within him; he hadn't noticed them before. He looked down at her back but couldn't see anything from where he stood. Quietly, she tugged the dress lower.

There, between her shoulders, was the result of being thrust against a photo frame that had shattered into her back upon impact.

He inhaled sharply, stifling the urge to punch through the wall of their rental. When he looked at her reflection in the mirror, he saw that she had turned away, her eyes lowered in shame.

Gently, he touched her with the tips of his fingers, acknowledging her torn flesh. He drew her carefully back into his arms. She leaned into him, though she still would not meet his gaze in the mirror.

He bent down and kissed her shoulder, then her neck, then the top of her head.

She turned and rested her face against his chest.

This was where he wanted to keep her.

DIARY: APRIL 10

Well, crap, Laurel. How did we get here?

You and I both know this is way worse than I'm letting on.

It's exhausting. I don't know whether to be grateful for the overwhelming workload that has forced my attention elsewhere, or curse it for siphoning away what little mental strength I have left for (relatively) meaningless fires.

Be grateful, be grateful.

And so I am. You know I am. You've taught me well to recognize the gifts—even amid heartache.

I'm trying to focus on the blessings, but my inner machinations are... askew. A wrench has been thrown into my depths, and I haven't quite figured out how to retrieve it. Compartmentalizing isn't working. I thought it was, but the night I woke up Chris (or did he wake me?) because of the nightmare, I realized I wasn't as okay as I thought.

I've been endlessly exhausted. Exhausted in a way I can't fully describe. I didn't realize I was having such intense dreams, but now it makes sense why I feel so utterly drained each morning.

I felt terrible for waking him, but the shame I still feel for allowing myself to be so physically and mentally affected by this... I HATE that. I don't want him worried or thinking I'm forever broken because of it.

So here I am, back to writing. If I get it out here, maybe I won't need to in my dreams.

DIARY: APRIL 12

—— ✕ ——

When we were in Florida, there was a moment of miscommunication that left me feeling defensive. I felt as if I needed to prove myself—not about what happened, but how, I guess?

Anyway, I struggled—HARD—with sharing the audio. I was afraid it was my only recourse to prove I wasn't lying (something my ex-husband, Joe, trained me to assume I always needed to do). Chris' response was basically, "No, I don't need to see it; I trust you."

Chris, who hadn't seen the bruises, the hospital report, the effects of the strong medications, the days after it all when I forced myself to exist through sheer determination—Chris saw NONE of that, and still he believed me.

To hear that trust so casually from him... it undid me.

I kept myself together until he went in to shower. Then I cried—not just because of what happened, but because of how badly I had allowed myself to be treated in the past, and how effortlessly Chris mended brokenness I didn't even know was still there.

He is amazing. Truly. In so many ways.

He is such a stark contrast to Joe.

I was married to Joe for nearly a decade. In the beginning, he love-bombed me relentlessly. I didn't know the term at the time, but looking back, the pattern is obvious. I had turned him down so many times that I think I became more of a conquest than a real person to him.

Once we were married, the effort stopped.

He knew my religious upbringing made divorce unlikely, and he behaved accordingly. He was confident I would never leave, no matter how bad things became. For a time, he was right.

To him, I was little more than a social accessory. I looked good on his arm and kept his life running smoothly. The house was clean. The laundry was done. Meals were cooked. Childcare was free. His contribution rarely extended beyond a paycheck because that's all he understood "husband" to be.

Cruelty was common, though rarely deliberate. Malice requires intention; what he displayed was something closer to entitlement. As far as he was concerned, I required no care beyond what served him.

If I was sick, it was inconvenient. If I pursued something for myself, it was selfish. If I tried to share something important to me, it was dismissed or met with accusations.

Any attempt to exist as a full person outside the role he had assigned me was met with belittling, frustration, and contempt.

Experiencing a mutually respectful and loving relationship has been absolutely jarring for me. I had spent so much time making excuses, explaining away hurt, and otherwise hiding my own mistreatment that I think I came to expect that a healthy relationship was impossible.

Chris has healed so much in me already, and I trust that together, we will heal this, too.

DIARY: APRIL 13

———— ✕ ————

I'm still exhausted. I'm in bed right now, but I'm having trouble sleeping. Writing used to help, but I don't know what to write about.

I guess I'm supposed to write about the assault. That's what's keeping me up, right? At least that seems to be the source of my dreams.

Can't I ignore it?

I guess during the day I can—so long as I sacrifice my nights.

What do you want me to say? What else needs sorting?

Florida was a big deal for me. I thought I'd handled the worst of it.

What a fool I was.

This weekend, I flew down to Kansas to see him.

In Kansas, something surfaced that I hadn't addressed. The last few times Chris and I were intimate, I wouldn't let him position himself behind me. It felt unsafe, and I chalked it up to needing time. I didn't dwell on it—maybe I should have.

This weekend, I teased him to the point of aggression. I momentarily stopped to grab a hair tie. I turned away from him, and he took advantage by hungrily plunging into me. He wasn't being mean or hurtful—he was doing exactly what I had built him up to do. I just wasn't expecting that position, and I was instantly terrified.

My body froze. I don't remember whether I spoke. I just remember being afraid and trying to convince myself that Chris had his hands on me. No one else.

I don't know how long we were like that. It felt like forever, but I know fear can distort time.

I think Chris realized I wasn't okay because he rolled me over to face him. Being able to see him made everything better. It took a minute for my heart to calm down, but I pushed the entire mess out of my mind until we were spent and content in each other's arms.

Chris acknowledged that we had "tripped over a landmine." I agreed, but I also recognized something new. My fear wasn't from the position, per se. It came from not being able to see him. I need to be 100 percent certain that HE is the only one touching me.

I can learn to find that assurance in other ways.

So even though it felt like a psychological sucker punch, it was useful. It helped me lay to rest another piece of the puzzle.

THE BEDROOM

To: Chris

From: Laurel

Hey love,

I've obviously been thinking a lot about you coming up in May, and I'm crazy excited about it. I'm pretty sure I'd be excited about meeting you in the middle of an active volcano, but I digress.

One thing has been gnawing at me, and I just want to put it out there.

I've only recently started sleeping in my own bed again. In the weeks after it happened, my bed stayed stripped. The sheets and duvet were taken, and I didn't really have anything else to put on it. I was both embarrassed and annoyed with myself for not being able to cross that mental barrier right away. I also fixed the photo frame that had been broken.

Point is, I'm sleeping in the stupid bed again, but I'm a smidge worried about sex there. I'm sure I'll be fine, but if I'm being honest, I've thought about it. I'm not worried that I'll turn you away or cry or otherwise react poorly. I imagine it would just be a temporary redirect of my psyche—like that moment in Kansas when you unexpectedly forced me to confront something I hadn't processed yet. And I'm not faulting you for that. I'm actually grateful you did what you did, because had you not, I might never have understood the "why."

I'm just trying to process things ahead of time so we don't stumble into another unexpected situation, you know?

I want nothing more than to feel you next to me every night—in that bed or any other one. So I promise I'm looking forward to you being with me there. And I'm looking forward to loving every inch of you with every inch of me. But I'm not oblivious to the elephant in the room, and I don't want you to be either. I mean… what are your thoughts? Do you even want to be here?

It's been on my mind, but not in a paralyzing sort of way.

I've also started writing in my journal again as a way to process all of this. I thought I had a good handle on it, but waking you up in Florida made me think twice. I still feel awful about that. I'm sorry.

I hope you're resting up. Please don't feel the need to respond to this right away. As I said, this was just something I felt I needed to float your way before you come up in May.

I love you.

DIARY: APRIL 16

———✕———

In my quest to move forward, I've forced myself to grapple with some things I had tried flatly to ignore under the guise of compartmentalization. Prime among them: my bedroom.

Since the assault, I haven't slept consistently in my bed. It took me a while to decide what to do about the bedding. That jerkoff took enough from me—he wasn't getting my bedding, too.

Looking at it that way helped. I reordered the duvet and sheets and redressed the bed. I forced myself to sleep in it more consistently. I'm mostly 100 percent back in my bed now, with maybe a night here or there when I fall asleep on the couch instead.

Progress, right?

Then there's sex.

Chris has been patient and aware, and I feel as if I've done a pretty good job pushing past the initial (what I'll call) rejection phase.

Going into Florida, I was petrified. I realize how awful that sounds, but I was SO afraid I'd make an even bigger mess of things. I was afraid Chris would recognize how hopelessly broken I was. I couldn't bear the thought of disappointing him. I STILL hate that idea.

But I went. And I went with my game face.

Luckily, Chris made everything as simple as possible for me. I knew if I could just get through that first time—not just endure it—things would be okay. Dammit, I was with Chris. I was going to enjoy him and make damn sure he enjoyed me. That bastard—again—had stolen enough time. The moment he entered my thoughts, I'd refocus on Chris... his face, his hands, his breathing.

And sex itself with Chris—even from the gate—has been fantastic.

I refuse to give up that level of satisfaction just because some asshat felt the need to prove something. Screw him. If I could endure terrible sex with him for 12-plus years, I could get past ten minutes of rape. Again—looking at it from this perspective helps.

I knew the horrible things Seth said to me weren't true. Joe would say similar things, especially when he struggled sexually. Never once has Chris blamed me or berated me or tried to shame me about sex. As a result, I haven't felt the need to avoid it. I enjoy it. And I enjoy HIM enjoying it.

But back to the task at hand... I'm not even sure how I veered off here. The whole issue of sex is obviously what's at play, but it was never really something I thought much about.

With my first serious boyfriend, it was awkward, exploratory, and fun—until it wasn't. That was my first foray into nonconsensual territory, but we were both so young, and I hadn't yet found my voice. I think I unfairly put a lot of blame on him when I carried plenty myself.

Then there was Joe. From the very first time we were intimate, I knew there were issues. I could tell he was embarrassed, so I never wanted to make things worse for him—especially after finding out he had written and directed an entire film sequence about how a former lover had berated him for the same.

I allowed him to blame me in a million different ways. I never spoke up because I worried that even a small blow to his ego would topple him. He admitted he had started taking pills from overseas while with his previous girlfriend. I begged him to stop because problems at his age were usually symptomatic of something bigger. He refused to see a doctor and instead allowed our sex life (if one can call it that) to nose dive into nothingness.

I tried everything—surprising him naked after a weekend trip, renting a motel room and dressing up as Princess Leia, sexy lingerie, you name it. I even tried injecting humor so he would get out of his own head.

I began to hate sex because it inevitably became a time for him to call me a failure—as a wife, a lover, a human. But again, I never let on that I knew his inability to perform had nothing to do with me and everything to do with him. I honestly think he recognized that and resented me for not "being the bitch." Being a horrible person would have made his shame easier, I imagine, because it would have been much easier to blame me.

Then there was Rick. I knew going in he wouldn't be more than a fling. He served that purpose, and I imagine I did the same for him. He was a fantastic kisser (like, DAMN), but our sexual styles were very different. But damn... epic kisser. 100/10. Would absolutely recommend.

Then Chris arrived.

We'd known each other for years, but a spark was lit on that trip to St. Louis, and everything changed. Everything. Thinking about that first time... it still gets my heart racing. Every part of me loves every part of him.

RE: THE BEDROOM

To: Laurel

From: Chris

We make connections to people, places, and things that often go far beyond our understanding. The more effort and thought we invest in something, the more value it accrues— whether we're fully aware of that process or not.

I'm not worried about what's going to happen. As you know, I tend to stay in the moment. If things go south, we'll deal with it. If we have to set the bed on fire and demolish the entire house, we'll handle it.

I can't fully predict how being in that room will affect me, but once we're curled up together and you're right where I can protect you, I doubt my worries will feel very large at all. The more I think about it, being there changes everything for me. My pain is that I couldn't protect you. That won't be the case once I'm there.

I'm glad you've returned to journaling. I've always found it to be the best tool for making sense of what's in my head— short of sitting down and talking things through with someone steady and sympathetic.

No apology required for waking me. I was only worried about you. I love you. I can't wait to see you, hold you, and kiss you. Loves.

DIARY: APRIL 17

———✕———

Last night, I pulled on Chris's shirt and went to sleep with St. Louis on my mind.

There was something wondrous about that first encounter.

You've got to realize that even beyond any sort of attraction, I love him. I always have.

We've been friends for more than 15 years. He's always been someone whose intellect and steady paradigm I've respected and appreciated. As for physical attraction, I'd never really looked at him that way. It never occurred to me that Chris was personally attractive. I mean, I'm sure I've told him he looked handsome in a suit and probably complimented him on something physical in the past, but how he looked never personally affected me.

The first time I had a real physical reaction to him was in St. Louis.

I'd already been divorced for several years, and he had moved to Kansas. We met halfway in St. Louis and planned to explore the city since I would be driving through and he had always wanted to see the Arch. We had only just begun discerning the possibility that our years-long friendship might be turning into something more.

The second night there, we'd gotten into our (separate) beds when I felt what I thought was a bug brush against my leg. I practically rocketed off the bed and tore the covers back to find it.

Chris looked over and asked if I needed him to kill anything, clearly amused at my apparent insanity. I was only slightly embarrassed (because c'mon—bugs), so I waved him off even though YES, I wanted him to KILL ALL THE THINGS.

He must've felt duty-bound to hunt down the phantom insect, because he rolled out of bed to investigate.

Holy sweet Lord.

He was only wearing boxers, and I got a glorious eyeful. I instantly felt myself blush and did everything I could to look at anything but him. After resigning ourselves to losing the elusive bug, we climbed back into our respective beds.

All I could think was: Crap. He's hot, too. Now what?

Even then, I was struggling with how to handle my sudden influx of feelings. Before, I had been able to rationalize everything as purely intellectual, but my body very clearly disproved that theory. So why not just sneak over to his bed? He's in boxers; he practically did the work for me!

I was still fighting myself. I could tell there was something between us, and I knew he was aware of it, too. But I LOVE him, and I couldn't bear the thought of losing him as a friend if things went south. So even if I admitted I wanted him—all of him—was I ready to risk losing him altogether?

I stayed in bed, especially since I wasn't entirely sure how he was handling whatever the heck this all was.

The next morning, we were using his phone to look up breakfast spots. I hopped into his bed to see the screen. He seemed noncommittal about the options, so rather than hover while he read through reviews, I slid under the covers (it was 60 degrees in that room!) and left him to decide.

Not two minutes later, he lay back down and positioned himself alongside me—almost, but not quite, spooning me. He wasn't as wrapped in the covers as I was, but I could feel the warmth of his body behind me.

I couldn't begin to tell you what we were talking about. My sole focus was his right hand. He had gently laid it on my hip, and as we talked, he'd softly move it to my waist or thigh. Every shift built more and more electricity inside me, but I didn't know what to do with it. I was beginning to feel an overwhelming need for him, so in an effort to preserve my own sanity, I cut off his hand's access by turning over. I hugged against him, desperate to redistribute the charge.

I sought out the sound of his heart. Strong. Steady. His hand moved over mine, and I felt safe... content.

Then—oh Lord, then—

He leaned down. I thought my hair was in his face, so I looked up, and as I did, he rolled his shoulder slightly so he could meet my lips with his.

I cannot properly describe that moment.

I was surprised. Anxious. Excited.

He was entertaining the possibility of this—of us.

That first kiss—he was soft... slow... tentative.

We broke apart, and I rested my head on his shoulder with a sigh of satisfaction. In that moment, I would have been content simply to breathe it in.

But he had only just begun.

I had barely settled against him when I felt his body shift. He positioned himself above me, and it was as though that gentle kiss had uncorked something deep within him. He wrapped me in his arms and pressed his mouth against my neck and chest. My naïve contentment vanished as urgent desire overtook every instinct within me.

My body rose to meet his—blankets be damned.

He leaned back, and I returned his urgency in kind. I wanted him—needed him—and since words felt irrelevant, the movement of my mouth along his neck, shoulders, and chest conveyed everything.

His hands found my hips and steadied me so I could feel the full effect my body was having on his. Feeling him move against me, knowing he was just as urgent for me as I was for him—my body registered every breath and sigh escaping him.

Words absolutely failed me. I pushed against him, impatient. He smiled, whispering restraint into my ear.

Then, without warning, he pushed into me as I cried out against his shoulder.

Oh, but he felt so perfectly masculine. So perfectly, perfectly masculine.

My apologies. This somehow turned into a dime-store romance novel, but now you can understand why St. Louis is my go-to happy place.

I still worry sometimes... What if he decides a ready-made family isn't what he wants? If moving home isn't best for him? If I'm not enough?

Trust is so hard for me. But I recognize the why, which makes it somewhat easier to shoulder. Open, candid communication is vital to me, and Chris has always been superb in that capacity. Sometimes I'm not sure how to handle it because I worry I'm pushing too much—but then he responds in a way that completely blows my mind. Just by being himself, he spoils me.

As such, I always try to do what little I can to show my appreciation and love.

I just wish he were closer. It would be a lot easier to shower him with affection without getting on a plane first.

DIARY: MAY 1

———✕———

The advocate still hasn't gotten back to me, and it's been months.

I've spoken to her once—ONCE—and the entire conversation was nothing but negativity. I don't know if she's inundated with other cases or what, but she didn't seem to think there was any point in my seeking anything beyond a Temporary Restraining Order (TRO).

She originally told me the TRO was automatically in place, but that's not true. I was then told that in order to apply for—and be granted—a Final Restraining Order (FRO), I would essentially have to endure a full trial. And because he is military, it would likely be denied because anyone with an FRO is automatically barred from owning firearms.

And as the lawyer so casually put it:

"The government spends a lot of money creating soldiers, and a soldier is no good without a weapon."

I can't even begin to describe what it felt like hearing that.

He SHOULDN'T have access to weapons. He met me twice—TWICE—and violently assaulted me while my kids were upstairs sleeping. Why? Because I bruised his fragile little ego.

Are you seriously telling me someone THAT emotionally unstable is who the government wants in a high-pressure combat situation? And why is their "investment" more important than recognizing and rectifying a grave injustice?

I'm just—

Why are women so easily cast aside?

Men complain about #MeToo and about feeling as though women are out to get them, and all I want to do is shake them. We wouldn't have to come together en masse like this if society didn't tacitly condone treating us as disposable receptacles for sexual frustration.

After that call, my hands shook for hours. It was as though my body registered something my mind still hasn't fully articulated. I'm just so done with this. So beyond done.

I think I'm going to reach out to Jenn tomorrow to see what insight she can provide, because at least she would understand the protocol for something like this.

Ugh.

Yet another person I have to bring into this crappy little circle.

TELLING JENN

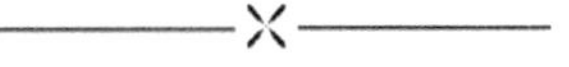

To: Jenn

From: Laurel

Hey girl,

I don't even know how to begin this, so I'm just going to lay it out.

A reservist raped me in February, and I've been dealing with the fallout ever since. I was told a TRO was automatically put into place and that he'd be held on base until the courts sorted out what was going to happen to him. Turns out that was a load of crap.

So I'm coming to you to see if you know what actually happens in circumstances like this.

Please know that I haven't shared this information with anyone beyond the tiny handful of people who absolutely had to know. I'm sorry to drop this into your lap—especially while you're planning a wedding—but you're the only person I know who might understand how this gets handled. All the information I've been given so far has been nonsense. Thanks!

— — — — —

Jenn immediately called Laurel.

Laurel wanted to ignore the call. She was at work and terrified someone might overhear. But she felt stuck. She knew Jenn could give her the information she needed.

Jenn was able to clarify Laurel's expectations, which alleviated some of her anxiety about next steps. Jenn was infinitely more helpful than the advocate who had given Laurel nothing but nonsense.

DIARY: MAY 2

I've been doing a deep dive into sex psychology—specifically rape. While it's been illuminating, it's also been overwhelming. I keep pushing forward, though. I tell myself that if I can just understand the why of what happened, I can ensure it never happens again. I can teach others how to avoid it. I can identify red flags. I can raise my boys into men who would never dream of such evil.

I recognize that this is a control thing for me.

I'm trying to intellectualize my way around a thoroughly emotional process. But I work with what I've got, and right now I feel like a spy lurking through places like Reddit, 4Chan, and even PornHub. Reading the comments. Seeing the content. Noticing which threads gain the most traction—and why.

It's horrifying what's out there.

I've flagged a bunch of content and forwarded much of it to a cybercrime reporting page. God only knows what becomes of that. It all just feels so... futile.

And I don't know that any of it has helped me understand why.

It has, however, alerted me to the sheer volume of men who actively engage in rape fantasies and boast about how much they'd love to hurt women. The level of anger, violence, and entitlement is staggering.

I worry for my own children.

How do I prevent them from becoming like that?

God help me.

DEMYSTIFICATION OF SEX

———✕———

To: Chris

From: Laurel

I've spent the last few weeks doing a kind of "demystification of sex"—though it's less about sex itself and more about the impetus for rape. I'll admit that my research has made me significantly more sensitive to what I'll call the masculine threat and, as a result, more empathetic toward women who are "in the line of fire." That's probably why our conversation soured last night.

I think you and I don't agree on what a "beta" is. In my mind, a beta is just a decent enough guy who isn't especially assertive or aggressive. When I say "basement dweller," I'm specifically referring to incels. We both know there is such a thing as toxic masculinity. You're on the normal, healthy end of things, whereas Seth is clearly not. You don't consume misogyny for breakfast; he does. You can tolerate a bruised ego; he cannot. You recognize that your strength can protect; he enjoys that his can exploit.

I think I get deeply uncomfortable with the whole male hierarchy structure. I don't know exactly why, but it makes me anxious—and it frustrates me that I can't quite figure out where everything is supposed to fit. Or maybe I'm just frustrated that it *does* fit, but not neatly, and so it spills over into other areas. And being the "everything in its place" sort of person that I am, I get antsy when things aren't in their proper place. I don't know. It's all very frustrating.

You're probably wondering why any of this even matters. Why am I looking into it? Why does it matter how alphas and betas are defined?

I guess because it's all I've got.

I need this to make sense so I can start reorganizing the men I encounter. I still feel uncomfortable around male friends, and that frustrates me because none of this has anything to do with them. Not really, anyway. I need definitions so I can categorize men safely.

And then that whole "Men and women can't be friends" video that Michel sent—it drove the fear home even further. He just thought it was funny, and I don't blame him. I can appreciate the humor on a surface level, but the fact that men openly mocked the idea that women could be anything beyond "sex potential" was alarming.

Both you and Michel confirmed that you mentally categorize women as "Yes sex" or "No sex." I'm not judging; I understand the biological basis for that binary. But do you see why I'm having such a hard time navigating all of this? I feel foolish admitting it, but I feel skittish all the time around men.

Even with Xavier and Michel (don't tell them that, because I'll feel like the biggest jerk in the world).

I haven't spoken to Xavier or really hung out with him in months. I was at Michel's house last week, but as soon as he got home, I left. He walked in, and I immediately said, "Okay, Sunny, I'll leave you guys to it!" and walked out the door.

I just... I can't.

And it's not their fault. I know that. I try really hard not to make them aware of my discomfort because if the situation was reversed, I'd feel horrible knowing they felt uneasy around me.

I can't help it, though.

There are a few male figures I don't feel anxious around, and I think it's because I recognize some form of physical superiority in myself in those situations. Rob, for example, is an amputee. I don't think he has an inappropriate bone in his body, but if I ever had to defend myself, I could— easily—against him. Because of that, I don't feel anxious. If I know I can physically defend myself, I feel calmer.

But I was getting antsy at Kyle's house. This example is going to highlight how messed up my brain is:

You were beside me most of the night. But there was a brief moment when you walked into the kitchen to throw away a candy wrapper and talk with Phoebe. I was instantly aware of my "aloneness" with Kyle—even though we were in a room full of people.

I would be lying if I said I wasn't anxious.

That's why I pointed out your physique to him as you walked out of the room. Yes, it was a joke—but it was also my way of reminding him: Do you see how large he is? Remember how large he is. And remember that I belong to him.

Now, I'm not saying Kyle needed that reminder. I'm not even saying Kyle would ever think of anything remotely inappropriate. Logically, I don't believe he would. But emotionally—psychologically—I feel the need to "show off the artillery," so to speak.

Am I making sense?

It's exhausting. I can't just be myself anymore. I feel as if I'm constantly on the lookout for enemy fire. And I FULLY realize how ridiculous that sounds—not to mention self-centered—but I was woefully underprepared before, and I refuse to be underprepared again.

So my pendulum has swung all the way in the opposite direction.

I'm aware of that, which is why I try so hard to act as though I'm not in fight-or-flight mode. I think having an organized, defined system for categorizing men would help. I've tried to come up with one—since my old one was clearly broken—but I haven't been successful.

I know this is something I'll eventually have to work through. It's just hard.

So yeah. I'm sorry for the novel.

I don't know that there's an answer to any of this. I just want you to know that I'm aware of my baggage—and that it colored how our conversation went last night. As you said, it's one of the ways we bump up against February.

I just don't want to be bumping against it forever.

Love you.

— — — — —

To: Laurel

From: Chris

I think the best way to characterize men is along two spectra: Competent (or Confident) to Incompetent, and Core Good to Malevolent.

True alphas would fall under Competent + Core Good. Seth would be Competent + Malevolent.

"Betas" would be Incompetent + Core Good.

And "Waste of Humanity" would be Incompetent + Malevolent.

As for you feeling anxious, this is what I was talking about when I suggested you might be dealing with PTSD—what I called "blowing out the whole structure." That said, I don't think you're in bad shape.

You're overcompensating for the paranoia. You don't trust your internal detectors because you think they failed you with Seth, so now they're turned up to 20 when they should probably be at 3.

But they didn't fail you. They did work properly. You just made some mistakes in logistics and in escalating warning signs.

Your body told you everything you needed to know. You were properly calibrated—you just ignored it for the sake of being polite.

Women are trained to be polite; we will not train our daughters to be polite.

I'm no shrink, but my guess is that you need to do two things:

- Spend increasing amounts of time with men you know you're safe around (Michel is a good example).
- Spend increasing amounts of time alone in relatively safe places—coffee shops, grocery stores, wherever—and actively compare what your gut is telling you to what's actually happening.

Naturally, right now both of those things are probably going to send you into anxiety hell. But you have to recalibrate, and this is how you do it.

You don't rebuild the structure by avoiding everything that stresses it. You rebuild it by exposing it to controlled stress and watching it hold.

I love you. I'm not going anywhere. And I trust your calibration more than you do right now.

Loves.

DIARY: MAY 8

He's coming tomorrow!!!

I'm still a little worried (a lot worried), but I have no doubt the worry will fade just being in his presence.

Work has been beyond draining. I'm being pulled in 30 different directions, and none of them are aligned.

It's also strange to realize how much energy vigilance consumes. It's like running a background program that never shuts off. Even when nothing happens, your system is still burning fuel.

I haven't been sleeping. I'm still not sure what the root cause is. I feel as though I've done okay compartmentalizing, but I worry I'm dreaming about things when I wake at odd hours... and maybe I'm subconsciously finding reasons to avoid bed?

I dunno.

I'm just beyond exhausted.

Soon... let him be home soon. Safely.

DIARY: MAY 9

He's finally home! For a little while, anyway. Trying not to think too much about that.

As far as sex goes, I'm okay. Mostly. It's a strange, unexplainable thing for me. Obviously, I love and trust him, but I still feel overcome with fear at times. I'm trying SO hard to force my way through those moments, and I can't tell if I'm doing a good job or if he's just being kind and pretending not to notice.

There were a few obvious moments when I simply couldn't get into the right headspace. And he was gracious and reassuring. But I know I HAVE to do all of this—I need to know I can. And maybe me pushing through is a horrible idea. I honestly can't claim to know. It's just all I've got, and I feel it's an important way to let him know I'm trying.

It's strange how things I thought I was okay with, I'm not okay with in my bedroom. I expected some differences—but not the ones I ended up with.

For example, he smacked my butt. He's always done that, and in Kansas, it wasn't an issue. In my room, though? The sound put me into a slight panic. I could feel myself freezing, and tears threatened. I was glad for my long hair.

Anyway, he smacked my butt only twice, and just the sound shot me back to Seth. I could feel him slapping me, and I began to shake. I kept willing myself to focus on Chris. His soft hair, his smell, his warmth—even hearing his heartbeat—it makes me feel safe again; it resets me.

I'm going to take advantage of him being here. I feel safe in my own bed. I haven't felt that way since last February. Not once.

Maybe I'll sleep.

DIARY: MAY 10

———✕———

The rest of Chris's visit was fantastic. Honestly, though, any time with him is fantastic. A few plans fell through, but we kept ourselves busy.

Unfortunately, sleep was elusive. I think I was so worried about waking him up with a bad dream that I willed myself not to fall asleep until my brain just gave out. The end result was me being utterly exhausted much of the time (though I tried my best not to show it).

My apologies for bringing up sex again, but that's what this is mostly about, right?

Sex this weekend was as it always is—until it wasn't. When things were compartmentalized, everything was fine, but there were times when I felt completely crippled. No, that's not true. I was paralyzed only twice. The other handful came in fleeting moments that, while difficult, rolled over me like waves in an ocean.

I'm still not sure what Chris feels about that, and I was frankly too embarrassed to ask.

The one time I know he noticed, he was responsive and reassuring. I had been trying so hard not to get too "heady" about things, but at one point, I suddenly felt very scared and overwhelmed. I couldn't get Chris to stop—he's big, and he knows I enjoy him being aggressive, so my initial physical response likely didn't land. I was trying not to ruin the vibe—I'm still anxious about Chris' perception of things—but I ended up blurting out, "I'm scared!" and he immediately stopped.

My adrenaline was through the roof. I couldn't stop shaking, and I was so angry with myself when I felt tears. I don't even know why I was crying—and it wasn't crying. A couple of tears squeezed out. I dunno. But he started talking to me, just reiterating that he loves me—that he's there—and I could feel myself calming.

As my body relaxed, he began gently resuming his motions, and soon nothing was in my mind but him. His thoughtful protection stirred something within me that... this is very hard to explain.

It felt healing.

Seth took from me—he wanted to punish and demean me so I'd feel as shamed and powerless as I'd made him feel. That's what psychologists say, anyway. Chris is clearly a stark contrast to that scumbag in so many ways. Beyond the obvious physical differences, Chris' treatment of others... his treatment of me... is light years ahead. I feel safe with Chris. Even from the gate, I was wary of Seth.

I just took a few minutes to think about this. If—God forbid—Chris ever squared off against Seth in an actual fight, I think Chris would win. His reach is longer, and he's taller, and I imagine his motivation for crushing him would be greater, too. Seth, while not short, is shorter than Chris. He is more solid, so that would be advantageous. He also has training and experience in combat—two things I hope Chris never needs. But even still, I think Chris' strength and size would quickly overpower him. That thought gives me quite a bit of satisfaction.

I'll likely never get to punch him in the face, but imagining Chris doing it? It's almost as good.

But wow, I just digressed. Sorry.

Point is, I had always felt I needed to be on guard around Seth. Even via email, I was wary in how I communicated.

Obviously, my almost 10+ years of friendship with Chris precluded uneasiness, but as I've reflected, it went well beyond just feeling safe. I knew that in his presence, I was PROTECTED. No one messes with you when your friend can lay them out.

Even that time in Cape May when my ex-husband got drunk and hit me—just mentioning that I had called Chris caused him to back down. The same thing happened when he threw me off our bed and shoved me onto the floor in the early days of our marriage. When he taunted me with, "What are you gonna do? Who are you gonna go to?" I said I'd call my brother, but Joe blew it off. Chris came to mind, and when I said HIS name, Joe got serious—somewhat angry—and then left.

It's a strange feeling to look back and see how I've always relied on Chris—even when he was COMPLETELY unaware of it. He barely remembers the Cape May incident, and I never told him about the bedroom one.

But my ex knew I had a good relationship with Chris, and though he'd claim otherwise, I know he would also recognize Chris as physically superior (superior in all the ways, really). Simply reminding him that I could call on Chris was enough to cause him to cool his jets.

How strange is that? Chris' mere existence, even thousands of miles away, gave me a measure of safety. That is crazy to me. I never really thought too much about it, but looking back, it blows my mind. And he never really knew.

I wish I could snuggle against him right now.

THE AUDIO RECORDING

Laurel had shared the audio recording with police. She also made sure the lawyer and advocate had copies. She had done her best to avoid listening to it, but the lawyer said something that caused her to spiral violently into the abyss.

He said, "The defense could easily paint this as role-playing. You are too calculated and don't sound scared enough."

She was too stunned to respond. She had already explained to him that she intentionally tried to remain measured in how she spoke because her children were upstairs. She didn't want to escalate things. The police who heard the same recording said they could clearly hear her "No," as well as the violence Seth had wrought.

How could the lawyer—the man who was SUPPOSED to be fighting for her—say something like that?

It crushed her. She left utterly defeated.

That night, she made the decision to listen to the recording.

At first, she couldn't listen to the whole thing—just a few seconds sent her anxiety through the roof as she curled into herself, a crying mess of brokenness. But she needed to hear what he heard. She needed to know if what the lawyer said was true.

It didn't make sense. Just hearing that recording sent her spiraling.

Unfortunately, it became an obsession.

She began having nightmares that extended far beyond the assault. She'd be in court, begging the judge to believe her, but everyone—from the lawyers to the judge to the jury—would say she was role-playing and trying to destroy a good, upstanding soldier. She'd wake in such a state each time that she would replay the audio over and over again to prove to herself that the nightmare had no basis in reality.

This created a horrific feedback loop that led to an increase in nightmares and a general deterioration of progress.

It took a few months for Chris to piece together that deterioration, as Laurel did her best to hide her struggle from him. She was ashamed, and she didn't want to burden him with what the audio contained.

This went on for months until one night Chris caught her when she thought he was still sleeping. He had flown up to visit, hoping to figure out what he was missing so he could better help her.

Laurel had awakened in a state of panic and, after confirming Chris was asleep, reached for her phone, plugged in her headphones, and replayed the audio several times. Little by little, she calmed down.

She wasn't crazy. She wasn't lying. She HAD said "No" to everything Seth had done.

Chris, however, wasn't asleep.

He had sensed something was wrong but decided to let things play out, hoping it would give him some perspective. When he realized what Laurel was doing, he nearly exploded with rage.

He grabbed for the phone, startling Laurel. She clutched it to herself and was suddenly faced with explaining the inexplicable.

He never yelled—he never even raised his voice—but the hurt, confusion, and pointed, "What the HELL are you doing?!" cut to the very heart of her. She could feel that he felt betrayed somehow, and it took her a moment to figure out why.

Oh God, he thinks I'm listening because I LIKE it!

Unfortunately, she was in such a terrible state that she couldn't speak. How could she explain what was happening in a way he would understand without admitting how hopeless she was? How broken she was—and always would be?

She was trapped, again, in that silent paralysis.

Only tears fell, but tears only served to drive Chris further into his own anger, confusion, and frustration. It was his job to help, damnit, but in that moment he wanted to set the whole house ablaze.

He walked out of the room and didn't return.

Neither one of them spoke that night. Neither of them could. Neither of them slept, either.

The next morning, Chris came back to bed and said that eventually Laurel would need to explain herself. Nothing made sense to him anymore, and he needed something—anything—to keep holding on.

She acknowledged his point and, since he was flying home that day, asked that he give her a chance to sort out her thoughts by email.

Chris begrudgingly accepted this, but only because he understood how important writing was to how Laurel processed things.

SILENCE AND PARALYSIS

To: Chris

From: Laurel

I still have trouble articulating my thoughts without writing them out first, so here's my attempt:

"I'm not ready to talk about it" implies there will be a time when I'm ready to talk about it; I don't believe that time will ever exist. And while I don't think you're charting my progress, I do feel compelled to show that I'm making the effort to put this behind me. That pressure doesn't necessarily come from you; I tend to do it to myself (that whole "NOW" part of my personality). How things shook out after you realized I was listening to the audio recording didn't help matters.

Please don't think I'm indicting you, because I logically understand we're both still trying to figure out how to navigate this. When you walked out, I felt punished for being paralyzed and silent. I knew you wanted an answer, and when you didn't get it, you left. I recognized that I hadn't made the progress you were expecting of me and, as such, I disappointed you. I hate disappointing you. I hate it more than I hate talking about this, so that should tell you something. Maybe you being disappointed with me isn't correct so much as you being disappointed with the situation—but to me, it feels the same.

And yes, we talked about it the next morning, but I'm still not altogether sure what I should be saying and what I should not be saying. You were very clear that you don't want to know what happened unless it pertains to us, but explaining the things that *do* pertain to us will inevitably paint the picture you don't want to see. I don't fault you for that, mind you. If I could surgically remove this from my head, I would. I certainly don't want to burden anyone else with it.

I try to be keenly aware of what I say or don't say, and when I'm unsure, I tend to freeze as I sift through the pros and cons—or I table it altogether until I'm able to sift better.

And maybe this is why you want me to talk to a third party. I can understand that. But can you understand why the thought of it suffocates me? Especially given the line of questioning that is inevitable? I don't know. It's just very hard to sort through, and as such, it makes more sense for me to stay silent. It's not me hiding anything; it's me setting it aside because I don't know if it's something that should be said or not. I tend to err on saying less because you can't take it back once it's out.

I don't know if I'm making sense. I can feel myself rambling again. I'm sorry.

But the audio is a whole different beast, and I'm still not 100% sure how to explain it to you without sounding completely crazy. I don't listen because I WANT to. I listen because I HAVE to. It's my way of proving to myself that what happened DID happen in the way that I remember it happening. Almost like a security blanket. A really effed-up security blanket.

I've been doing it for months, and I realize it's causing more problems than it's helping, but it's like a compulsion now, and I don't know how to break myself of the habit.

I just don't know what to do.

I'm sorry.

— — — — —

To: Laurel

From: Chris

I feel confident enough in saying this was my poor reaction driven by past experience. I've always encountered silence in a "Chris is getting screwed shortly" manner. I don't take kindly to it. So, in the moment, my reaction was to punish you. I wanted you to know this was bad behavior and wasn't going to be tolerated. Then I left, and I seethed, and I tried to wrap my brain around everything.

I realized, "Maybe she can't actually talk."

Basically, I've trained myself to react that way, and when you subverted my expectations, I had to reevaluate the situation before I could act correctly. I don't think that's either of our faults, but I did need to make adjustments to account for you. In these situations, it's my job to figure out the best path forward. I made a misstep, recalibrated, and tried to rectify it the next morning. I'm just sorry you carried the burden for that.

I don't know how to fix your feelings about me being disappointed in you. Nothing could be further from the truth. You've gone above and beyond what most would have in your situation. I've always known you to be tough as nails, but you're in a class all your own, love. Is there progress to be made? Of course. It's one of the reasons a psychologist would prove helpful—more on that later. But I'm interested in hearing what YOUR benchmarks for progress look like.

As far as the assault, I want to know as little as possible. There's a difference between "you need to know this so you'll understand" and "completing the whole picture." I don't need the whole picture. But if we're struggling through something and I need to know something to clear it up, tell me. I can handle it. I know this isn't the clearest demarcation, but I don't know what you know, so I can't make the call on what is too much. I think the simplest test is: "Does Chris need to know this to understand the current thing we're sorting out?" Let me know if that makes sense.

Regarding talking to a third party, I want you to do so because you will be forced to deal with all the things I can't force you to deal with. Yes, you can journal and try to work yourself through it, but at the end of the day, no one is holding you accountable. You can find little rational tricks to avoid thinking about things. You can disguise your feelings and put things under the blanket of "it's best for X if I do Y." You can listen to a fucked-up audio and cause more nightmares for yourself and convince yourself it's normal. A trained third party will eat that for lunch and keep you on the path. And you will have someone to talk to who doesn't have a vested interest in anything other than you being better.

You did everything right and STILL didn't see justice. THAT will blow out your foundations. You need professional help from a trained psychologist to rebuild them.

— — — — —

To: Chris

From: Laurel

I think part of the issue is neither one of us knowing what progress—real progress—is supposed to look like. My benchmarks for progress (regarding this) are:

- Sleeping through the night consistently
- Relinquishing control of the audio recording on the phone
- Being able to catch and diffuse triggers without anyone noticing
- Pushing through uncomfortable or anxious situations

Basically, I'm progressing when I continue to be who I am and live my life as I wish in spite of bleeding out now and again because of the penknife in my leg. Yes, it's there, and it hurts, and it's frustrating—but it can't kill me. Owning that and living it out is progress.

What does progress look like to you? Do you have benchmarks in mind (beyond throwing my phone into the ocean)?

Also, thank you for reevaluating and making the adjustment in your response that morning. It took me a while to fully unpack that entire experience, and when I finally did, it scared me how close I felt to the edge of utter chaos.

Like, I think this is how multiple personality disorders happen.

The scary part is I could feel my mind splinter off. I heard you talking, but I couldn't hear what you were saying. I just felt your voice reverberate through your chest against my back.

What I COULD hear were various splintered versions of me yelling at each other. There were three of us—one was like a drill sergeant, screaming at me to soldier up and take control of the situation. Then there was Victim Laurel, who was crying and telling me not to listen to Drill Sergeant Laurel because her directives were dangerous. Finally, there was Passenger Laurel—the "me" both Drill Sergeant and Victim Laurels were yelling at.

In my mind, I could see all three of us riding in a car. Drill Sergeant was driving. Victim Laurel was trying to grab the wheel. Passenger Laurel (who I think was the real "me") was in the backseat between the two of them, sort of just waiting to see who won the fight. I had zero care as to who ended up in control because, regardless of who won, I knew without a shadow of a doubt that we'd end up driving off a cliff.

At some point, I remember you saying, "Laurel, come back to me," and all three Laurels stopped and turned to look at you.

Suddenly, the three Laurels weren't in a car anymore but in an ocean at night. Obviously, my back was still to you, but in my head, Passenger me suddenly felt like driftwood being pushed back your way by Drill Sergeant and Victim Laurels, who were completely silent.

It was the strangest sensation to go from overwhelming noise to utter silence—to go from being pulled in two directions by clearly opposed forces that suddenly united to push me in one direction.

And I realize I'm going way more in-depth with this than I should because I probably sound insane, but I guess I haven't unpacked it as much as I thought I had.

I noted in my journal later that I understand better why split-personality disorder can be caused by trauma. It's so hard to explain because I was simultaneously fully in control and fully out of control. I recognized who I was, but I also recognized—completely distinct from myself—the Drill Sergeant and Victim Laurels. But as distinct as we were from one another, we were completely the same as well.

Flippin' trippy as hell.

And I still don't know that I necessarily have a handle on it. Looking back, it still scares me how close I felt to losing myself completely to this fracturing.

Though now that I'm writing it out to you, I'm beginning to see a bit of id, ego, and superego at play. Superego would be the Drill Sergeant. Victim would be the id. Passenger would've been ego, I guess. I dunno. Rambling at this point. I guess I'll have to revisit this.

Please don't think I'm nuts. It was probably the worst I've been since the hospital in February, and given the circumstances, I doubt it'll happen again. At least I'd sincerely hope not, because holy hell. That was not fun.

But I guess regarding your point about seeing a third-party psychologist, you raised something I hadn't thought of. And just as you said, I immediately started typing out a defense that was little more than "it's best for X if I do Y." Blah.

Again, I take your suggestions very seriously, but I admit struggling with this one. It's not that I don't see merit; I just don't see the benefit outweighing the cost. I'm making progress on my own, and I fear rehashing this with someone else is going to set me back again.

I like not waking up in a panic every night. I like not freaking out about various sounds in the house. I like not being afraid to take the trash out at night. I like being able to order food again because I'm not afraid of hearing a knock on the door after 5 p.m. I like having terror-free sex with you.

I'm not perfect—I get that there's still progress to be made—but if I start talking to someone about this, I'm worried I'll slip right back into all the stuff I struggled so hard to get past. I don't want to go backwards.

As far as accountability, if things ever reach a point as they did with my brain splintering into different versions of myself, I'll be the first to sign up with a psychologist. For now, writing it all down is a means to keep me on task.

But I will say that your point about not seeing justice has blown out my foundations? You're 100% correct.

When Joe got all macho upon realizing what had happened, I rolled my eyes and said, "Please. He might've left physical marks, but what you did was a million times worse." And in both cases, I won't see a lick of justice.

I can handle what others do to me. I don't like it, but I recognize their actions speak more about them than they do about me. I refuse to allow their actions to dictate my self-worth. However, when I go out of my way to do everything right and things STILL blow up in my face, I have a really, really tough time with that.

I am a very justice-minded person, so when I'm denied it, it really does blow out my foundations.

That said, I've never needed professional help rebuilding those foundations before, and I don't think I need it now.

TALK WITH RYAN

---×---

While Laurel tried to assure Chris that she didn't need a psychologist, the incident with the "multiple Laurels" had scared her. She also knew that relying on the audio recording was a problem, but she wasn't sure how much of a problem.

She decided to talk things over with a friend—a licensed therapist who had his own practice. However, since he was not aware of what had happened, she framed her questions as, "Help me help a good friend."

Ryan's response was fascinating.

He explained the psychological concepts of "flooding" and "systemic desensitization," which he believed this "friend" was engaging in. It was a way for her to feel control over what had happened because she had the power to start and stop the recording whenever she wanted. She could process it however she liked.

He cautioned, however, that such psychological techniques—when not employed under the watchful eye of a trained therapist—often led to substance abuse, because many patients struggle with the intense emotional fallout from such a heavy-handed approach.

He likened it to an allergist helping someone overcome an allergy. The allergist can slowly introduce an allergen to a patient, increasing exposure incrementally until the patient builds up tolerance—all the while watching for an overwhelming reaction, at which point the allergist would employ medication to stop it.

Patients attempting to do such a thing on their own may not know what warning signs to look for until it's too late. Thus, he recommended that Laurel ensure her "friend" was connected to a trained clinician as soon as possible.

Ryan also mentioned that this was a form of "cognitive restructuring." That phrase gave Laurel something to research, and she poured herself into it.

RE: SILENCE AND PARALYSIS

———————×———————

To: Laurel

From: Chris

Your benchmarks align with what I see in my head. The phone thing isn't like "the ring that binds them all," but the more I think about it, the more it *is* like that.

I don't think you're nuts for the multiple-personality thing. It's a fairly common concept in psychology. As far as the psychologist goes, my main concern is that by not going in reverse and dealing with the consequences now, you may be making it harder for all of us in the future. Not that I suspect you're doing that willfully, but it's entirely possible.

Neither of us is a trained psychologist. We're just swinging and seeing what we hit. And while I respect your thoughts on this very much, we don't agree. Whether or not that becomes a problem remains to be seen. For now, it is not—and for now, that's enough for me.

Regarding your comparison of justice between Joe and Seth, the latter's marks were more than physical, love. They were immediate, whereas what Joe did was long-term, giving you time to adjust to his myriad disappointments.

Both scars will linger, doubtless, but Joe's will impact the boys more than they impact you. Seth's are yours to carry and sort. Obviously, I'll help, as will those you let into this circle. But ultimately, you are the one who will bear the weight most acutely.

I TALKED TO RYAN!

To: Chris

From: Laurel

I talked to Ryan! He was able to give me a lot of really good insight into the audio recording portion of things. He said that I was subconsciously flooding my brain with the trauma in an effort to desensitize myself to it. "Flooding" is an actual psychological technique that helps with what he called "systemic desensitization." He did warn me that doing this can lead to substance abuse, but I don't know what universe that would be an end result for me. Regardless, he mentioned that systemic desensitization should happen in conjunction with cognitive restructuring.

I had to look that up after we talked. Basically, it's training your brain to redirect negative thoughts and associations by identifying them appropriately and realigning them with reality or a more optimistic point of view. You can also replace the associations by creating new associations, but it takes conscious effort. At least that's what the internet is telling me. Regardless, I realized that I can also replace the audio recording with other things. Maybe instead of immediately reaching for the audio recording, I instead play videos of the boys or of our trip to St. Louis. I recognize this is a habit, but habits can be broken. Maybe I just need to create a new habit.

Anyway, it did make me feel a lot better to know that what I'm doing is actually normal. I really thought I was going off the deep end, but apparently, this is likely what they'd attempt to do in therapy. Now that I have a name for it, I can look into it further and see if I can't put together a plan of attack. I hope this makes you feel a bit better, because it certainly makes me feel better! Love you!

— — — — —

To: Laurel

From: Chris

That's fantastic, love. I'm glad you finally talked to someone who knew what they were talking about—and it didn't kill you!

Please consider doing this for real and not just "for a friend." I think you'd gain so much from the experience if you'd just give it half a chance. I'm going to look into this stuff, too. I want to understand it better, because this has been a challenging one for me to process—and if I'm not processing it, I can't help you.

I'm proud of you for reaching out to him, Laurel. I know this is hard, but you're doing so much. You don't have to do it all on your own.

Loves.

TEXTS: THE PSYCHOLOGIST

———✕———

Chris: I've been thinking a lot about this, and I really think it's time you at least tried to find a psychologist.

> **Laurel**: Why? Because of a few bad dreams? Or did the multiple-personality thing freak you out more than you care to admit?

Chris: You and I are both smarter than that. At the very least, you should have a professional who can help you sort things out and hold you accountable when your clever little brain makes excuses.

> **Laurel**: That's why I have you, Michel, and Sunny.

Chris: We're all smarter than that. I want you to at least promise you'll try talking to someone with expertise in this area. For as much as Michel, Sunny, and

I want to help, we aren't professionals,
and you will probably gain better insight
from someone who has helped others
find their way. If it doesn't work, it
doesn't work—but I think you owe it to
yourself to at least look into it.

Laurel: I reached out to Kiera,
remember? She had training along
those lines because of her time as an
RA. I'm pretty sure she's experienced
her fair share of assault drama to date—
especially now that she and Steve live
on campus. We know how swimmingly
THAT went.

Chris: Doesn't count, and you know it.
Especially since she probably never told
Steve what happened out of respect for
your privacy.

Laurel: Welp, not that it matters
anyway. I wouldn't want to step
between a husband and wife, and I
think Kiera felt really uncomfortable
talking to me. I love her and don't want
to make things difficult. Better for me
to just fade into the ether.

Chris: No, better for her to step up and
be a friend—but that's just me.

> **Laurel**: Meh. If it'll make you feel
> better, I'll give it a go. But I'm telling
> you now that I'm only giving it four
> sessions. I feel that's more than fair.
> One to do the administrative "How
> much do you hate your father?" stuff,
> another to discuss the actual issue,
> another to go over possible treatments
> or insights, and a final one to see if
> anything came of anything. Deal?

Chris: I think that's fair as long as you
keep an open mind. Don't just go in with
the expectation that it's going to fail.
And make sure you get someone who
actually specializes in assault and PTSD. I
really think you have PTSD.

> **Laurel**: Noted. I promise I'll give it a
> fair shake. I've also checked out some
> online support groups that may prove
> useful. We'll see where the path takes
> me.

NEW HOUSE

While Laurel was juggling work, motherhood, and healing, she was also juggling the purchase of a new house.

On paper, it made sense. The location might open better educational options for the boys. The layout felt lighter. The bedrooms didn't carry echoes. And when Chris eventually came home for good, this would likely be the house he'd move into.

It felt like progress.

It looked like progress.

But she couldn't ignore the questions underneath it all: Was she building a future—or just a distraction? What if she was mistaking motion for healing?

Staying in the current house felt suffocating. But trauma doesn't live in drywall; it lives in the nervous system.

Maybe a new house would offer a clean start. Or maybe it would just be a prettier place to carry the same unhealed wounds.

She honestly didn't know.

DIARY: MAY 11

———————✕———————

Effing A, already!

I'm still not sleeping. I constantly go to bed after 1–2 a.m., inevitably waking with my heart racing at a thousand miles per minute. Then I can't fall back asleep.

How can I function?

It is too much, Lord. Please.

And then everything at work is exploding. And the housing stuff. And the financial stuff. And the academic stuff for the boys. And the continued lack of parental competence from Joe.

I'm so overwhelmed. So very overwhelmed.

I need to be able to sleep. Just one night. What can I do? Writing isn't helping as I thought it would. Am I writing about the wrong stuff? What do you want? The stupid dream?

NO. NO. NO!

Isn't that worse anyway?

I HATE ALL OF THIS.

ALL OF IT.

It's all so much worse when you know. It's why I don't knowingly read or watch books or movies with upsetting endings. Clearly my brain doesn't GAF about that. Whatever it's trying to tell me, I don't f*cking wanna know.

But maybe that's the price I pay for sleeping?

Help me. I don't want this... please.

It always starts the same.

I'm with Chris, and we're watching a movie. I hear a knock on the door, and I know it's him.

Chris is gone—I don't know where—but I know the boys are asleep upstairs, and I can't let Seth come in. I try SO HARD to push the door closed, but he's too strong.

He is so angry. I can feel hate roll off him, and I move to block the stairs. I hope Chris is with the boys because I know I'm about to die.

I'm scared. I don't want to die. I don't want to leave my babies. But I know he intends to kill me, and I cannot stop him.

As such, I do not scream or try to throw anything at him. I don't want to wake them. I don't want them to see their mother raped and murdered. I don't want them hurt by him.

He smiles at me—a lion smiling at a mouse.

He wants to make me feel powerless. He wants me to beg for mercy, but I'm not stupid. He's going to kill me regardless. Begging would only give him greater satisfaction, and for as scared as I am, f*ck him. He wasn't getting that.

My defiance makes him angrier. He slaps me across the face, and I crash into my desk. I try not to let anything fall—to stay quiet.

Before I can pick myself up, he grabs my arm and pulls me to my feet. Using his other hand, he yanks my head back by my hair. Then he pulls my robe backward and pushes me onto the bed, trapping my arms.

As I struggle to free them, he hits me again, hissing at me to stop. I ignore him.

He rips my gown and starts biting my chest—hard. I have to bite my lip to keep from screaming; it hurts so much. He roughly shoves his fingers inside me, but I finally manage to free one hand to push him away.

That only makes him angrier.

He begins to choke me, stopping only to slap me as he tells me what a worthless, stuck-up bitch I am, and how I—

WTF?! How does this help?! How does writing any of this down help?!

DIARY: MAY 12

Sorry.

I can't do this. I tried. I don't know what else to do, but it can't be this. I was up ALL NIGHT after that.

Just... no. There has to be another way.

I've tried ignoring, compartmentalizing, talking, typing, and now writing. What else? This all threatens to suffocate me, but I REFUSE to let this crap win.

NO. NO.

Help me. Please. I'm begging You. Help me.

I'm back. I had to take a few hours after that.

I'm really upset. I was supposed to call Chris earlier but opted to text instead, which I think frustrated him. Better for him to be frustrated than to feel helpless, I guess. I dunno. I feel as if all my choices, regardless of intention, have been wrong.

I am exhausted, overwhelmed, and overly emotional.

I spent a good chunk of tonight cleaning Sunny and Michel's house—the one useful thing I've been able to accomplish. Again, I just need sleep. Everything is so much worse because I can't sleep.

I wonder if I'll ever sleep again.

Maybe when we move and I'm not in this room anymore. I'm so tired.

So tired.

DROPPING THE CHARGES

———✕———

After a particularly distressing meeting with the lawyer—and having had zero luck pinning down the advocate—Laurel was faced with a decision: pursue the charges, knowing it was unlikely she'd see any form of justice while enduring the trauma of a trial, or drop everything and feel like a failure for letting Seth get away with it.

The lawyer made it very clear that she was fighting a losing battle. He cited, again, that Seth was a soldier. He said her audio recording could easily be brushed off as role-playing. He pointed out that the rape kit, while containing Seth's DNA, was inconclusive because Seth had admitted he was there but claimed everything was consensual. And worst of all, he noted that a trial would force her to discuss the most private details of her life—not just pertaining to Seth, but to any past or present relationships.

To Laurel, it felt as though the trial process was designed to torture those who came forward. It was HER life that would be laid bare and HER privacy that would be violated. She still hadn't told most people what had happened, and a trial would place her name into the public record. It would inevitably force her to tell people she did not want to tell—her family, her friends. She feared, intensely, that they would forever treat her with pity or even anger.

And worse still, the boys would one day find out what had happened.

It all felt like too much—especially knowing the odds were against her walking away with any sort of victory.

So, through tears, she agreed to drop the charges.

It crushed the life out of her and planted a heavy guilt in her chest. What if he did this again to someone else? Would it be her fault because she failed to fight until he was behind bars?

She again flirted with the idea of suicide—but ultimately refused to sacrifice her sons' emotional stability for a "what if" that might never come.

She couldn't talk to Chris for several days afterward. In fact, she didn't talk to anyone for more than a week. She locked herself in her house and existed on cereal and *Doctor Who*.

DIARY: MAY 20

———✕———

I dropped the charges.

I feel like the worst person in the universe, but I dropped the charges. The lawyer insisted I'd fail. The advocate's non-response told me all I needed to know about how she felt regarding my chances of success. And since I have two boys who need their mother whole—not further broken by a trial that would eviscerate what little sanity she had left—

I walked away.

I am so scared he's going to do this again. There's no way you will convince me I was his first victim. I may be the one he escalated furthest with, but who knows? I made sure my evidence is part of his military record and that police kept everything I gave them in case he is caught hurting someone else. At the very least, it will enable whoever comes after me to build a better case. But I keep praying there won't be anyone else.

I'd like to think this scared him straight;but since he won't face real consequences, it might embolden him.

The thought crossed my mind to kill myself.

I haven't admitted that to a single soul because, almost as soon as it settled in my mind, I rebelled and forced it into an "Absolutely Not" box. It wasn't as strong as the urge for self-immolation I had in the weeks immediately after February, but I convinced myself it might be the best way to protect future women from him.

If I could amass all my evidence in a tidy bow and write a letter explaining what he did—and why I felt suicide was my only option to ensure his name was forever associated with rape—then maybe he'd never have the chance to hurt anyone else again.

But then I thought of my boys.

They don't deserve to lose their mother because our justice system is trash.

I mean, what the hell? Our justice system is so broken that I actually contemplated taking that drastic measure as a means to protect potential victims. Why am I taking on that burden when we have a system in place that's supposed to do that?

It's all so messed up.

I realize this isn't my fault and that I'm operating within a system stacked against me. I hate this so much. I REALLY hate that my advocate was the worst "advocate" in the history of advocacy.

I'm going to write a letter to the agency to let them know she ought to be removed from the program because she did piss all for me. Her lack of advocacy hurt me terribly and set me up for failure. She gave me incorrect information that put me, and my boys, in real danger. Luckily nothing came of it, but damn—how does she look herself in the mirror knowing she's not doing her job?

I find her more abhorrent than the lawyer, who—while a dick—was mostly just relaying his experience trying to prosecute cases like this.

I hate everyone and everything right now. Myself most of all.

I don't know that I'll ever stop hating myself for being unable to move forward with this.

I HATE feeling like I had no other option.

God help me, I hate everything.

LETTER TO THE ADVOCACY GROUP

———— ✕ ————

To: Whom It May Concern:

When I found myself in the emergency room being processed for sexual assault, I asked aloud how I was supposed to move forward. How was I going to juggle the legal ramifications, work, life, and all the chaos in my world that felt like multiple grenades exploding around me?

The nurse who processed me said, "Don't worry. You will be assigned an advocate, and she will help. She's trained to walk with you every step of the way. You'll never be alone."

Her words felt like a blanket around me. Having someone who knew how to navigate the impossible ocean of fear, uncertainty, and pain I had suddenly been thrust into felt like a gift. I left the hospital that night hurting—but hopeful.

An advocacy program. What an amazing idea. Setting up survivors of assault with a personal guide is brilliant. There are so many moving parts to juggle, so having someone who understands not only the legal pieces but also the trauma and healing pieces? I loved it.

Unfortunately, my advocate (if one can call her that) was a travesty. Thinking I had her to rely on—at all—probably hurt me more than it helped. I was rarely able to reach her. She gave me incorrect information on multiple occasions. She flat-out told me she didn't believe I would ever see justice. And then she essentially ghosted me.

I'm not sure if she is still with your organization. I hope she isn't. But if she is, she needs to be retrained or let go. If she is not, I suggest your organization develop a better policy for redistributing caseloads so people like me do not fall through the cracks.

The program you supposedly run sounds wonderful on paper. I never got to experience it, so I cannot say whether you actually do what you claim to do. I pray I am an outlier—some strange anomaly that others who have benefited from your program cannot relate to. I want this program to flourish. It NEEDS to flourish, because God knows how many women need you. But you will succeed only if you have the right staff in place.

I understand this job is extraordinarily difficult. It must be emotionally taxing on a scale incomprehensible to most. The stress I've endured over the last few months would topple Atlas, so I can only imagine how fatigued your advocates must feel juggling multiple cases. Please do not think I am throwing shade out of spite or malice. I am trying to make you aware of how damaging it is to survivors to be paired with an advocate who does not actually advocate.

It was demoralizing to hear her repeat—more than once—that I would likely never see justice. I know the statistics. I did not need someone supposedly on my team reminding me of them. I needed her to motivate me to try anyway. I needed her to remind me that reporting him and pursuing charges was the right thing to do because it could protect future victims. I needed her to tell me my struggle was not in vain.

She also provided information that was simply incorrect—information that very well could have placed me and my children in harm's way. When I asked about a restraining order and how to obtain one, she told me that, because he is military, one is automatically in place temporarily. That is not true. She also mentioned he was grounded on base until the investigation was complete. I later learned that was not entirely true either.

Do you know how terrifying that is? I have children. I believed I was at least partially protected by a restraining order that never existed. While he may have been held on base briefly, he certainly was not required to remain there "through the investigation."

Worst of all was how impossible it became to reach her. I believe I spoke to her three—maybe four—times. Then she disappeared. I did not know what to think. Did she give up on me because my case was not a slam dunk? Did I ask too many questions? Did she leave the organization? Get hit by a bus? Win the lottery? I have no idea. And I still have no idea.

The nurse who first told me I would have an advocate made me feel that, even though I had been thrust into a violent storm, I would have a lighthouse to guide me through it.

The advocate was supposed to be that lighthouse. She was not even the mirage of one. A mirage, at the very least, would have offered hope.

I implore you to better vet your advocates, provide stronger training, and offer continued counseling or supervision if you do not already. The task you are asking them to perform is not easy. But the work they are supposed to do is vital.

The idea behind your organization is brilliant and desperately needed. But in my case, the execution of your mission hurt far more than it helped.

I sincerely wish you success. So many women are counting on you.

Sincerely,

Laurel

SOLICITING THE PSYCHOLOGIST

———✕———

To: Dr. Heart

From: Laurel

My name is Laurel. I am a survivor of sexual assault and am currently navigating the aftermath in a way that is deliberate, honest, and largely self-directed. My partner has encouraged me to explore therapy; and while it has never been a modality I felt particularly drawn to, I have agreed to approach it with an open mind.

I want to be transparent from the outset. I am already deeply introspective and willing to confront difficult material without avoidance. I am not looking for hand-holding, nor do I need assistance locating or articulating my thoughts and emotions. What I am trying to determine is whether therapy can offer something additive to the work I am already doing—rather than merely replicate it.

To that end, I find it helpful to establish clear expectations. In my mind, four sessions would be sufficient to assess whether this is a productive fit. Ideally, those sessions would include: one to review relevant personal history; one to engage directly with the trauma itself; one to discuss the secondary effects I am experiencing; and one to reflect on the healing process I have already undertaken.

I understand that healing is not linear and is rarely tidy, but having a loose framework and a defined evaluation window will help me assess its ongoing usefulness in a grounded way.

If you have availability and feel comfortable working within these parameters—or discussing how they might reasonably be adjusted—I would welcome that conversation. If not, I completely understand and appreciate your candor.

Thank you for your time and consideration.

Sincerely,

Laurel

DROPPED CHARGES

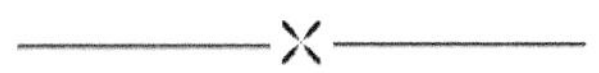

To: Chris

From: Laurel

I still feel terrible about last night. I made a bad decision, and I'm sorry for it. Even though I had reasons, they were not, as you said, "enough" to justify not calling you right away. So again, I am sorry and won't wait to reach out with things like this in the future.

There are a couple of things that came out of that conversation that I want to highlight:

- You feel as though I do not trust you.
- I think you may distrust me now (regarding whether I'm telling you pertinent information).
- I think you feel as though I've quit (regarding the charges).

Rather than allow these to simmer on their own, I want to address them, because this situation leaves me feeling very precarious.

You feel as though I do not trust you.

Forgive me if I'm beating a dead horse—maybe this was already resolved via text—but please know that I *DO* trust you implicitly. My decision had nothing to do with trust. I was trying to protect you from worry, anger, frustration, or feeling helpless. I also wasn't sure I could handle myself on the phone in that moment, which would have made everything sound even worse.

You were the first person I called when I finally felt capable of having the conversation. This is difficult for me. It's not that I don't want to talk to you; it's that until I feel sorted, I can't.

Think back to what happened in Florida. Now imagine my calling you in a full panic but being unable to articulate what the issue actually was. Your mind would have pinged like a pinball machine—covering everything from a horrible accident involving one of the boys to Seth returning to God knows what else.

That said, I could and should have texted you. I thought I was helping, but I wasn't. It made telling you later that much harder. I won't make that mistake again. I'm sorry. Truly.

I think you may distrust me now.

This might be projection (self-fulfilling prophecies and all); but if I were in your shoes, I'd probably wonder, "If she didn't tell me X, what else isn't she telling me?"

If that's where your mind is, please let me put it to rest. There is nothing regarding this situation that I haven't shared with you—barring, of course, what you asked me not to share. There are deeper layers you're unaware of, and I'm not always sure how to navigate how much of that awareness you want or need. But that feels like a natural tension in situations like this.

I'm trying. And I know you're trying. Even if we're not at 100%, I still believe we are light years ahead of many couples who have faced something like this. I'm not a crying ball of victimhood fully clothed in a cold shower.

You're not some unhinged caveman retreating into yourself. That matters. Please recognize that. Please recognize that I am trying, too.

You can ask me anything. I will answer honestly. I always have, and I always will.

You think I've quit (regarding the charges).

This physically hurts me. I honestly believe you think I made that decision on a whim dictated by fear.

Yes, fear played a role—but it was low on the totem pole once I had time to process everything. My focus has been fractured for months. I tried to push this forward, but it's hard when the advocate doesn't return calls and the lawyer tells you it's pointless. I even had Ron (who knows her through church) reach out. Nothing.

So I consoled myself with the possibility that they truly believed this wasn't the "slam dunk" I thought it would be—that they needed to focus limited resources elsewhere.

Do you think I *like* that? I hate it. It makes me feel worthless, even though I know that's not the intention—it's just the system.

I wrote a pointed letter to the advocacy program. If I couldn't make a difference through a court case, I can at least attempt to influence the paradigms of those walking victims through the process. This cannot stand.

This isn't quitting. It's recognizing reality and consciously choosing to mitigate inevitable hardship for the boys and me while still effecting some small measure of change. I'm doing what I can in a broken system. I'm not doing nothing.

With that said, I've been reflecting—a lot. I've been writing, trying to excavate the background baggage that drives my more subconscious automations.

For example: at my son's party, I was sitting with Sunny, Michel, and Mary. Mary complimented the house. I joked about getting it ready for sale. Michel said something implying he wouldn't know the difference. I responded, "Oh, that's right—you've never been to the house, have you?"

Sunny and Michel looked at me like I'd lost my mind.

A few minutes later, it hit me. Of course he'd been there. He watched the boys the night I went to the hospital.

That realization shocked me. I knew I compartmentalized well. I didn't realize I did it so thoroughly that I could temporarily forget something that significant.

I've been trying to determine whether that defense mechanism is good, bad, or neutral. I still don't know.

The same pattern shows up elsewhere. Joe constantly accused me of lying. I've been conditioned to assume others think I'm lying, too. I feel the need to prove myself constantly. I recognize where it comes from—but I don't recognize it in the moment. Only afterward.

Please know I am trying. I need you to understand that. I even started poking around in online support groups!

This is hard on every level. I'm trying not to complain. I'm trying not to give you additional reasons to worry.

And I do trust you. I value your opinion. I reached out to Sunny and Michel because you suggested it—not because I felt compelled, but because I take your feelings seriously. I don't know if you believe that, and that bothers me because I don't know what else I can do to demonstrate how much I value you.

When you said you wanted to see whether your trust in me would change, it felt like, "Either shape up or this won't work." That hurt. In my mind, this had nothing to do with trust. I understand your perspective, which is why I apologized and will not repeat the mistake. But it still hurts that your instinct was to distance yourself and place the onus on me to fix everything.

This is a situation neither of us asked for, wanted, or has experience navigating.

So here it is. A hundred pages of rambling. And somehow it still feels insufficient.

Don't ask me to reassess my trust. My trust is already decided. It always has been.

Please don't think I'm angry. I'm not. I just need to know where we stand. And as you know, I prefer to ask directly.

ONLINE SUPPORT GROUP

Susan: I'm really upset right now and needed to vent. As someone who was raped, I already have to deal with enough every single day. I don't ask for much from people, but tonight I wanted to go to a concert and I didn't want to go alone. Being a survivor means things are harder for me than for other people, and I thought my bestie would understand that.

I asked her multiple times to come with me, and she kept saying she couldn't because she has a headache and work in the morning. A *headache*. I'm sorry, but when someone you care about has been through trauma like mine, you show up. You push through discomfort. That's what support looks like and I told her that. It just feels really gross that she's choosing sleep and work over being there for me. I gave her multiple chances to come correct after I pointed out what she was doing. I e-mailed, I texted and I even called her to leave a voicemail so she fully understood how she was making me feel by not coming. She ignored me anyway and chose her bed over me.

I didn't choose to be assaulted, but here I am, still trying to live my life, and it would be nice if the people around me would make an effort instead of acting like minor inconveniences matter more than my trauma. I shouldn't have to beg my friends to show up for me. If you can't be there for a rape survivor when she needs company, maybe you shouldn't call yourself a friend at all. So I sent her an e-mail telling her I didn't need that kind of friendship.

Eight years down the drain because she couldn't be bothered to come to a concert for me. I'm just so disgusted with her.

Julie: I'm so sorry. People who haven't been through trauma just don't get how hard it is to ask for support. A headache is temporary—your healing isn't.

Jackie: Honestly? If she were a real friend, she'd suck it up and go. Trauma doesn't run on a schedule, and work will always be there. You deserved support in that moment. You gave her a bunch of chances and she dropped the ball. It sucks, but you were right to walk.

Carli: This is exactly why survivors feel so alone. Everyone says "I'm here for you" until it actually inconveniences them. I'd be rethinking that friendship, too, especially if you tried to explain yourself more than once. She can't pretend she didn't get how important this was to you.

Yvonne: You weren't asking for anything unreasonable. You were asking for companionship and safety. If she can't show up for that, that says more about her than you.

Tonya: People love to talk about supporting survivors until it requires even a little bit of sacrifice. I'm angry on your behalf. You shouldn't have to beg someone to care.

Shay: I'm glad you didn't minimize your needs to make others comfortable. You are allowed to need people and take up space. If she couldn't do this one small thing, I'd let her go, too.

Laurel: I want to say this gently, because I know how charged these conversations can be, and because I believe survivors deserve honesty as much as compassion.

I am concerned with the way this situation is being framed. Our trauma does not entitle us to override other people's boundaries, nor does it turn discomfort, illness, or exhaustion into moral failures. When someone says "No," regardless of reason, that "No" still matters.

You said you tried multiple times to change her mind. Your trauma does not entitle you to her "Yes." It concerns me that many of us here seem to be excusing the use of pressure and guilt to try to change her friend's "No" into a "Yes." Coercion doesn't become healthy just because it comes from pain. In fact, many of us were harmed precisely because someone believed their needs outweighed our right to refuse. We should be especially careful not to replicate that dynamic ourselves.

Support does not mean unconditional compliance. Friendship does not mean sacrificing bodily autonomy. And healing does not come from teaching ourselves, or each other, that boundaries are negotiable if the feelings are big enough. You absolutely deserve care and compassion; we all do. We also all deserve to have our "No" respected - on every side of the conversation.

Susan: To everyone who commented support and validation, thank you.

To Laurel... Wow. I am honestly shaken by your awful tirade, and I'm not sure how this is being allowed in a group that is supposed to be safe for survivors.

Your response is invalidating and frankly harmful. You don't get to police how other survivors process their trauma or what support looks like for them. The fact that you felt comfortable lecturing a rape survivor about "coercion" and "boundaries" is disgusting. You are exactly why so many survivors stay silent.

This group exists to SUPPORT survivors, not to dissect their reactions and accuse them of being "dangerous" or "unhealthy." That's not allyship.

Honestly, this comment made me feel attacked in a space that's supposed to be about empathy. If this is the kind of response that's going to be tolerated, then this group is no longer safe. I really think the admins need to step in here, because this kind of shaming has no place in a survivor support group.

Jackie: OMG, seriously. Expecting that your friend be your friend by coming to a concert is not the same as expecting you're owed sex. Admins need to remove you. You are clearly not a safe person. You don't attack a survivor like this. What is wrong with you? We're here to validate and support each other, not dictate what another person's healing should look like. You're making a bad situation worse. She doesn't need your negativity. None of us do.

Laurel: Blind agreement is not validation and it is certainly not supportive. Blindly affirming every reaction may feel comforting in the moment, but it can and does excuse coping mechanisms that are ultimately harmful to ourselves and to others. Real support includes reflection, accountability, and the willingness to sit with discomfort without lashing outward. Lambast me all you want, but my goal here was to point out that coercion is coercion regardless of who or why. At the end of the day, coercion is not something any of us should be comfortable with utilizing or excusing.

Laurel was promptly removed from this online support group after her post.

DIARY: ENTRY 14

———✕———

I'm taking the dates off these entries. I read that, for things like this, dates can make it worse because they force us to think about progress linearly—as if I shouldn't still be struggling three months later instead of evaluating things entry by entry.

We'll see how that goes.

I told Chris about dropping the charges a week after I did it. What a mess.

He was angry, disappointed and hurt. Obviously my intentions completely missed the mark. No matter how thoughtful and aware I try to be, I still suck at this, and I feel awful.

Worse, his response set off a giant red flag for me. I'm feeling VERY vulnerable right now—as if he could discard me at any moment. I can't tell if that's my insecurity or if I'm actually reading him correctly.

I spoke to Sunny and Michel. Surprisingly, I was chastised more by Sunny than by Michel. I also reached out to Xavier (who came to help with the house inspection). I hadn't intended to tell him, but when he asked how Chris was, I got upset. To assure him Chris wasn't the problem (per se), I told him about dropping the charges.

He gave me the most Xavier-esque hug to date, which made me smile. I genuinely love him beyond comprehension. Again, I love my friends, Lord. I appreciate them more than they will ever realize. Please allow me to be useful to them in some way.

I think I just need time—free of everything.

Alas, that is impossible.

So I'll keep swimming.

I need to, for the sake of my boys.

You must wonder why I don't write about them more often. In truth, this whole book feels like one giant record of mud, bile, and tears. I hate the idea of putting anything of them in here. They are sunshine, and joy, and everything good and perfect in the world. I don't want that sunshine and joy mixed with this muck.

I'm going to try to sleep now. Wish me luck.

RE: DROPPED CHARGES

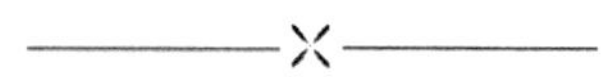

To: Laurel

From: Chris

I'll admit, I wasn't expecting this email today. I was of the impression that we had sorted everything out. I apologize in advance that this will be a brief response.

To your points:

- "You feel as though I do not trust you"
  After clarifying the situation with you, I am less concerned about this than I originally was. I believe you when you say that you understand my perspective and that you will not do this in the future.

- "I also think you distrust me now"
  This is not my line of thinking. I trust you to tell me the truth in all cases, until you prove me wrong, which I doubt you will. What happened in Florida stuck with me. The lengths that you went to prove your honesty was telling.

- "I think you feel as though I've quit"
  My concern was allayed after you clarified the whys. A non-response from an advocate and an in-conclusive kit leaves you with practically nothing, and I understand that in the context of the legal system.

I have been thinking that I've been too hard on you. After all, you're navigating the chaos as well as you can, and I don't want to increase your burden. But this is really quite important to me that you keep me informed so that I can keep the ship on course (damnit, we're stuck with these sailing metaphors), and I believe you understand that. We are a team, even if we are separated by half a continent.

I'm really glad you talked to Sunny & Michel about what is happening. Seriously. Thank you. And I know how hard you are trying, believe me. The fact that you are addressing these things of your own accord speaks volumes.

I hope this calms your fears regarding us, if not, please tell me. Loves.

— — — — —

To: Chris

From: Laurel

Thanks for responding. I appreciate you doing so even though you had to be brief.

I'm glad trust is intact, and I'm glad you recognize I wasn't just giving up on the charges. I'm going to take a few days on this, though.

Which, hey, that works out well! Enjoy your trip to Seattle. I can't wait to hear all about it!

— — — — —

Chris: Got your e-mail. I suppose that's
not unreasonable, but could you at least
clarify what needs taking "a few days" on?

Laurel: To keep with the analogy, I no
longer feel I'm on the boat, and I can't
decide if that's because I'm in the dingy
or if I'm in view of the plank.

I love you. That hasn't changed (nor
will it). I just feel very... precarious.

Chris: To keep with the analogy, you're
in the captain's quarters.

Laurel: I now have a very vivid desire
to role play peeling you out of your
captain's attire in those quarters...

...to find a ship to borrow for a few
hours.

Chris: Wait, are we talking Captain
Kirk, or Captain Hook?

Laurel: I was originally thinking ocean,
but let's be honest... I'd enjoy peeling
you out of just about anything.
Anywhere. Space, sea or otherwise.

Chris: And I would enjoy you doing the
peeling, babe.

DIARY: ENTRY 15

——— ✕ ———

So housing stuff keeps imploding. I'm beginning to believe God is pushing me away from Springfield for whatever reason.

Chris seems relatively indifferent. It's difficult finding time to figure this out. He's going to Seattle for work, so maybe then? I dunno. I feel as if everything is out of my hands anymore. Sunny is worried I'm jumping the gun a bit w/ Chris, though (and I laugh as I say this) her husband stands to lose his future BFF if I bow out of a relationship. In all seriousness, though, while she recognizes the validity of my concerns, she feels Chris, himself, is unaware of how his responses to me might need better clarification. Again, I dunno.

I'm just beat. In all the ways.

On the productive side, I did find a psychologist who specializes in PTSD and sexual trauma. She's nice and seems to understand my desire to be efficient during the four sessions I have with her. I vetted several psychologists with similar backgrounds, but this one stood out because of the care she took in addressing my concerns with my introductory email.

The first session went as expected. Lots of general background information given and a brief description of why I was in her office. I was honest about that, too. I explained that while I believe therapy is important and transformative for many people, I just didn't think I was a good candidate because of how I've always processed things. I was there because Chris asked me to give it a try. I hope I didn't come across as a giant jerk.

To her credit, she didn't waste much time with what I'll consider "administrative stuff" before getting into the nitty gritty, so bonus points for that. I was NOT a fan of her "guided meditation" thing, but Chris said to be open, so I went along with it even though my soul felt like clawing its way out of my body to punch me in the face. We shall see.

ANOTHER ONLINE SUPPORT GROUP

Tom: My therapist that's been helping me with life and some childhood sexual assault stopped practicing therapy. I searched her name, curious as to why.

Turns out her kids were killed by her husband! So even if she started therapy again, knowing this, should I even use her? I personally don't care about her stuff as long as I reach my goals and if she can do the job. I don't want to start therapy with another therapist because it would take 6 months to get to where me and her are, but wow.

How long do you think it'll take her to come back to therapy? Do you think she'll be able to help me anymore, or do you think she'll be too messed up from her own stuff? Should I just find a new therapist?

Laurel: You need to find yourself another therapist, STAT. This woman lost her children in a truly heinous way, and your main focus is how this impacts YOU.

You definitely need a therapist and it definitely should not be her, now or whenever (if ever) she feels like entering the therapy space again.

Clare: I agree that he should try and find a new therapist. While his post did come off as a little self-interested, you came off judgemental and mean. Finding a new therapist is hard, definitely after spending lots of time gaining trust and comfort. I think you should have worded this differently to be more understanding. Shaming someone will never result in change. Let's keep this a safe place.

Laurel: I validated his need for a therapist and answered his question about if he should still use the therapist in question.

I also pointed out that his response to this woman's tragedy was self-directed.

Was I direct? Yes. Is me holding a mirror up to his words "unsafe?" No.

Hard truths and accountability are the keys to true healing.

I also really wish we'd stop conflating "comfortable" with "safe." Healing isn't comfortable. Accountability isn't comfortable. Truth isn't always comfortable.

But all of those things are necessary if we really want to progress towards healing. I wish that for the OP and genuinely hope a new clinician is found.

Respectfully, your chide of "unsafe" is just a means to squash any challenge to comfort, not to promote healing. I want people to truly heal.

Laurel was promptly removed from this online support group after her post.

DIARY: ENTRY 16

I may or may not be the dumbest person ever. I realized I could FINALLY surprise Chris! He traveled to Seattle for work, so I asked for his flight info. Knowing his return flight meant knowing exactly where and when he'd be home!

Guess who is sitting at the airport now waiting for him?

Hopefully we can figure some things out. Again, this whole long-distance relationship thing can take a flying leap.

DIARY: ENTRY 17

———✕———

So HOLY CRACKERS, I've got so much to catch you up on. You'll never guess where I am...

FREAKIN' OKLAHOMA!

We were en route to visit Kristyn and her family when I asked what he would've been doing had I not flown in. "Gone to Texas," was his response. "Just for a drive."

?! That's more than eight hours "for a drive." But hey—why not?

So after visiting Kristyn and going to Target for some clothes and toiletries, we're going to Texas. We're almost there but crashed for the night at a SUPER shady motel. Chris is out cold in bed. Poor guy is exhausted. I am too, but I needed to get this whole mess off my mind.

When we arrived home from the airport, I immediately initiated sex. That wasn't my intention at first, but upon realizing his disposition—game on.

As usual, everything was fine until it wasn't.

He laid me back, and I was SO ready to have him (these weeks apart have been beyond frustrating). But he didn't move over me the way I expected. Instead, he positioned us in a way that mirrored how Seth had tried to.

He has no way of knowing. And I have no way of telling him—I cannot, cannot, cannot. Of all the things... no.

I tried to go with it, but I felt a scream rising from deep inside me. I could feel it climbing from my belly through my lungs. I was fully aware of how precarious my grip on self-control was—and of the losing war I was waging to keep it.

Given how unsure I still felt about where Chris and I stood, I was doubly desperate to stifle the memory that position triggered.

I feel like an idiot, but here I am—crying in a motel bathroom—because that moment felt just as bad (if not worse) than... I can't. Please.

Anyway, with what little strength I had left, I asked as casually as possible for him to get on top of me. I have no idea whether he sensed my panic, but he obliged. We soon moved to his bedroom, and everything settled after that.

I don't know what to do about these... other moments. I'm not sure how to manage or avoid them without upsetting Chris (not the right word, but I'm tired and can't think of a better one). He's been very clear about not wanting to know details—and I'm fine never sharing them—but if I react with fear, he'll eventually piece together what Seth did based on how I respond.

That's why I try so hard to head off any extreme reactions or play things off. He doesn't want to know, so I want to control myself better. I just don't know how.

And as if that weren't enough, Chris decided to discuss my trepidation about our relationship. Honestly, it was probably for the best—but I was unprepared. I'd expected that conversation at the end of the trip.

It turns out he hadn't intended for his email to land the way it did, but even his explanation put me on alert. I again felt as though he was waiting for me to admit—even in some microscopic way— that I enjoyed what happened.

I can't stand being in my own skin just thinking about that. And his suggesting it—even unintentionally, even as a fear— makes me physically sick.

I can't. I feel sick and upset and angry and—I can't.

I don't ever want him to say or suggest or mention that possibility again. Not as a "maybe." Not as a "what if." NO. On no planet. In no circumstance.

NO.

Okay. Took a minute. Sorry. I'm tired. I should sleep, but I'm worried I'll wake him.

I hate when I get like this. I hate not being able to articulate myself and feeling broken. He eventually realized I wasn't trying to be difficult, so he wrapped his arms around me.

Truth be told, I felt l as if I were covered in acid. I didn't want him to touch me. I hated how I felt in my own skin, so feeling his arms against me made me want to shove him away.

"Escape" feels accurate.

But I didn't.

I knew he was trying, and he needed to feel as if he was helping just as much as I needed to feel okay. So I stayed and let the acid press deeper into every pore. I thought I might suffocate from the heat burning through me, but I stayed and focused on his voice.

Steady. Firm. Decisive.

Slowly, the acid drained. It still hurt to be touched, but by then he had settled, too, sensing he'd "done his job," so to speak. I went to the bathroom for tissues and space. Just a few moments.

In those moments without him, though, I realized I wanted him back. I'd rather endure heavier pain with him than lesser pain without him.

So I curled back against him—content and steadier than before.

He is my anchor. I feel more stable with him.

Now I'm ready for bed. Can't wait to curl against him.

DIARY: ENTRY 18

Texas was a blast! We weren't able to do everything I'd hoped, but we managed some fantastic adventures nonetheless:

- Bungee jumping (because Chris is crazy)
- Some centrifuge thing (for us, because he makes me crazy)
- Reunion Tower
- Thanksgiving Square

We hit up a few terrible diners, too. Honestly, I think the best part was just driving around. There were stretches where we didn't talk at all—and that was fine. We definitely wandered down a few conversational rabbit holes, but I genuinely enjoy simply being with him.

He didn't get annoyed with me even once for touching him. I still wonder sometimes if he just lets me do it because he knows I enjoy it, but I don't know... more than sixteen hours in the car together, and not once did he seem bothered.

I'm trying to take that at face value, but it's hard. My ex-husband used to get annoyed with me for that because he was self-conscious about dandruff, so having free rein now feels strange. I don't want to overdo it and frustrate Chris, too.

But again—trust, right?

He says he likes it. So maybe God is being His typically kind Self and paired me with my tactile equal.

The rest of our time together was fantastic, too. It just gets harder and harder to leave him.

Lord, please get him home safely—and soon. I'm anxious to have him beside me every night and morning.

DIARY: ENTRY 19

—————✕—————

Uuuuuuuuugh.

I really, really, really, really, really hate these appointments with the psychologist. I feel terrible saying that because she's nice and genuinely seems to want to help, but I almost feel as if I'm guiding her through the how and why of where I'm at.

This isn't her fault, mind you. I've had more than a year to process this crap. And it's not as if I'm the typical client who struggles with introspection or connecting the dots between id, ego, and superego. It drives me crazy that I'm paying upwards of $200 per session to walk her through how and why I arrived at my thoughts and feelings.

Her suggestions so far have felt pointless. Again, I try not to fault her too much—I'm sure these things are helpful to others—but telling me, a person who has journaled her entire life, to "start writing your feelings" or "keep a dream diary next to your bed" makes me want to stab things.

She suggested today that I "challenge my perception of masculine/feminine power dynamics," and I nearly screamed.

CHALLENGE MY PERSPECTIVE?!

Lady, do you understand that I've challenged my perspective six ways to Sunday and, within the last year alone, arrived at a WHOLLY DIFFERENT UNDERSTANDING of the male/female dynamic???

Challenging my preconceived notions is practically my hallmark. I relish that level of self-reflection because it sharpens and solidifies my views—or forces me to abandon them for something better.

I do not want to spend $200 per session just to be told to do things I'm already doing—and have likely been doing longer than she's been a therapist.

Again, she's nice. I think she wants to help. But this feels pointless. I am capable of navigating this on my own. When I need help, I go to the people who can give it: Chris, Sunny, Michel.

I think I'm going to talk to Chris about bowing out. I tried. I really did. At this point, it feels like a waste of time and money.

I also had a bit of an epiphany regarding my healing journey the other night.

Long story short, I was reminded of Myla and got overwhelmed missing her. Not a day goes by that I don't think of her. I realized in that moment that just as I still mourn my daughter—and will every day for the rest of my life—I will carry this scar with me for the rest of my life as well.

I've put so much pressure on myself to heal, heal, heal that I don't allow space for lifelong emotions to ebb and flow.

One of the dumbest examples is this very diary.

When I decided to start journaling again, I intentionally bought a separate notebook from the one I use for everything else. I didn't want this crap commingled with happier life memories. My intention was to burn this book once I finished it, and I gave myself only one year to "get it all out." I thought imposing those parameters would force me to confront everything efficiently.

Instead, I put undue pressure on myself and missed recognizing my own progress because I was constantly falling short of the arbitrary deadline I'd set.

Worse, I intentionally chose a small, compact journal, which only compounded my anxiety as I neared the end of its pages.

I remember Chris telling me just to get another book. I was so frustrated that he couldn't understand why doing so would feel like admitting failure.

Poor Chris couldn't see how many of these boundaries were supposedly "beneficial."

Turns out, we probably should have met somewhere in the middle.

Ah well. Hindsight is 20/20.

BREAKING UP WITH THE PSYCHOLOGIST

————✕————

To: Dr. Heart

From: Laurel

I doubt this email comes as a surprise, but I feel guilty nonetheless. I talked things over with Chris, and we both agreed that I gave this an honest try. I don't feel as though our sessions have had much effect, so I'm having a hard time justifying the cost.

I don't fault you for that. As I mentioned before, I don't think therapy is particularly beneficial for someone like me. What I need most is time—and permission from myself—to process things. Instead, I've been giving myself arbitrary parameters that make no logical sense, and failing to meet those illogical expectations has been the source of much of my frustration.

Rather than continually moving the goalposts, I'm working on removing them altogether.

This is probably TMI, but I hope it helps illuminate where I am so you'll understand when I say I've got this.

I suffered a miscarriage in 2013. Her name is Myla Thérèse. I think of her every day. It took me about a year to speak about her with anyone outside the five people who originally knew. But once I gave myself the space and time to process my grief, I was able to heal genuinely and carry her memory with grace rather than constant pain.

This weekend, I encountered something that reminded me of her in a particularly painful way. I acknowledged it, processed it openly, without shame, and moved forward.

As I reflected on that, I realized I should approach my assault the same way. I'm not ashamed of still carrying grief for my daughter years after losing her—why would I be? She's my daughter. I will always love her, and I will always miss her.

The same applies to my assault. I'm allowed to grieve the safety and bodily autonomy I believed I had before it. I don't know why I felt I forfeited that right simply because a year had passed. The parameters I imposed on my healing—intended to accelerate progress—ultimately did more harm than good. They were helpful early on because they motivated me to confront difficult material. But like anything, there is a point of diminishing returns.

I no longer need artificial deadlines to compel me to do the work. What I need now is space—and self-permission—to process without the constant pressure of "Why aren't you healed yet?"

The assault, like my miscarriage, is a scar. It does not have to remain an open wound, nor does it have to be crippling. There will be moments that trigger emotions related to both experiences. Rather than becoming angry with myself for feeling them, I intend to acknowledge them as part of being human.

Please know that I genuinely appreciate your time and effort. I would happily recommend you to others. For now, unless I find myself in need of a "tune-up," as you so aptly put it, I'd like to discontinue our sessions.

Thank you again for walking through this mess with me.

Sincerely,

Laurel

— — — — —

Laurel: I broke up with Dr. Heart. I sent her an email tonight.

Chris: And you're sure this wasn't just a bad match?

Laurel: Oh, it was a bad match—but not because of her. Therapy itself just doesn't work for someone like me. I'm convinced of it. I'm glad it works for other people, but I'm not one of them.

Chris: Why do you think that is?

Laurel: You said it best the other night. I don't have the time or the desire to futz around with Seasons 1–30 of my life just so a therapist can trust me when I say this doesn't stem from some unresolved, long-forgotten conflict with my father, mother, or dog.

Chris: Just because you're capable of
sorting yourself out nine times out of
ten doesn't mean you can't use a little
help for the one in ten. Yes, therapists
need to do some archaeology at first,
but you don't have to relay every detail
from birth.

Laurel: It feels that way, and it irritates
me to no end. I don't like feeling as
though I have to trust someone who
hasn't earned it. She wasn't a bad person,
mind you. I just felt it was a waste of time
because her suggestions only highlighted
how little she knew me. I don't fault her
for that—how can you really know
anyone in a couple of sessions?

This is why I prefer discussing this stuff
with people who already know me—
people who've done the "archaeological
work" of who I am.

Chris: She's trained in this, though.
None of us are.

Laurel: You don't have to be. I don't need anyone to tell me the way out. I just need someone to listen while I sort it out myself. I need accountability and the occasional heads-up that I'm veering off course. My circle knows me well enough to recognize those things. A random therapist does not—and cannot.

Chris: I think you don't really understand the role of a therapist.

Laurel: Maybe. But I really did try. That was our deal.

Chris: It was. I just wish it had worked better for you.

DIARY: ENTRY 20

———✕———

I've been thinking a lot about the arbitrary goals I set for myself. At first, they were helpful. They gave me a sense of control when I felt I was spiraling. But as Chris pointed out, they eventually became a burden—they had outlived their purpose. I convinced myself I needed them to stay motivated and effective, but I am naturally motivated.

Besides, I have Chris and the boys. I want to be the best version of myself for them. I'm also, admittedly, spiteful, and I refuse to allow trash like Seth to hold power over me.

So while it's been difficult to relinquish some of the parameters I put in place, reflecting on which ones are useful and which ones are not has been, in itself, a healing exercise. Inevitably, I learn something about myself and my process. I've always believed I was thoroughly introspective, but this experience has taken that to an entirely new level—and it hasn't always been pretty.

That's okay. I prefer honest to pretty.

I feel as though I've seen myself honestly in ways I never had before. This kind of experience forces you to grapple with darkness. The hardest part is recognizing that the darkness is part of you.

At the same time, when you claim victory even if it comes broken and bleeding you gain a strength that cannot be manufactured any other way.

And Chris will be home soon.

We'll get married, find a house, make it a home, and fill it with beautiful babies, music, and laughter. His presence brings peace—and so much joy.

I thank God every day for the grace to persevere.

I know my rainbow is ahead.

DIARY: ENTRY 21

———×———

Welp, I was removed from yet another support group today because I refused to pretend that trauma alone makes every action righteous.

I've come to believe that many of these spaces are not actually about healing; they are about preservation. So many people guard their trauma, terrified that if it's examined too closely, it might lose its power.

But I cannot accept the lie that healing means never being challenged—that we're always right or forever exempt from accountability simply because we survived tragedy.

In these groups, "support" has come to mean unconditional affirmation. Every feeling is validated. Every reaction excused. Discomfort is labeled harm; accountability, violence. And God forbid you suggest that trauma may explain behavior but does not justify it—you're deemed "unsafe."

"Unsafe."

I swear that word makes me want to spit. It has been hollowed out beyond recognition, repurposed as a pejorative to bludgeon others into silence.

I've watched people use their victimhood as leverage—to guilt friends, to coerce compliance, to demand exceptions from basic social norms. I've seen boundaries dismissed as betrayal and consent reframed as something other people owe you if your pain is big enough.

When I tried to name that, I was attacked and removed—again and again. But blind validation is not compassion; it is stagnation. It teaches people to orbit their trauma rather than move through it, rewarding dysregulation and punishing reflection. It offers temporary comfort at the expense of real healing.

Healing is not the same as being agreed with.

I have never been one to pretend that clinging to something is the same as honoring it. I want more than survival. I want integrity. I want healing that doesn't require me to abandon common sense.

Sigh.

I recognize that my direct approach can be jarring—unpalatable, even. My tone and words were gentle, but my message was not. Apparently, that was violence.

I can't eyeroll hard enough sometimes. But then I remember: they are struggling to find their own path to healing, too.

Grace, Laurel. Grace.

I just don't know how to approach serious situations timidly. Real hurt requires real healing. I don't understand those who would rather tap dance around problems than charge through them. I truly believe it is harmful—not just to the individual, but to society.

Please, Lord, never let me fall into that. The idea of using my trauma as a crutch, an excuse, or a badge of honor makes me physically ill.

TOUGH CONVERSATIONS

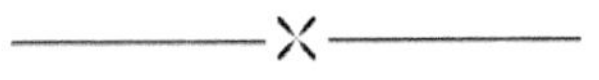

I'm really glad we had that conversation last night. I know we've already discussed this, and we seem to be more aligned, but I wanted to reinforce a few things:

There's a distinction between the brokenness of a whole person and the brokenness of a specific aspect for which that person is struggling.

For example:

- I fix broken algorithms in a product that otherwise works flawlessly.
- I generally function well in life, but my diet is clearly a mess.

I do have reservations about your ability to separate what is actually your fault from what you merely perceive to be your fault.

Regarding the article about the man who repeatedly and creepily pursued a woman after she told him she wasn't interested: I meant that strictly in a legal sense. By the laws of the land, he's entitled to make a complete asshat of himself. It's the responsibility of the rest of us to correct him.

I think you may ascribe a more negative interpretation because of your experience with Seth and how quickly things escalated from bad to worst-case.

***

To: Chris

From: Laurel

I'm glad we talked, too. I was honestly nervous about having that conversation over the phone. Writing feels safer to me because I can articulate my thoughts more precisely and revise as needed. Speaking doesn't afford that same control. Still, I decided it would be a good challenge. I knew you'd be steady—you always are with this sort of thing—but this is an area I want to improve. So, thank you for letting me practice on you.

Regarding the distinction between whole-person broken-ness and aspect-specific struggle: your analogies make sense. Given your reservations about my ability to separate truth (what I'm actually responsible for) from fiction (what I merely feel responsible for), I can appreciate the distinction.

I really am trying to get better at this. But it's hard. My instinct has always been to shoulder responsibility, regardless of whether it's truly mine. I genuinely believe in the adage, "The buck stops with me." Of course, there must be caveats—but I struggle to see them in the moment. I have to reflect consciously and assess culpability, which is difficult because my default setting is to absorb blame. Breaking that habit is not easy. So while I may balk when you say, "That wasn't your fault," I promise I sit with it later and evaluate whether you're right.

Regarding the "creepy dude": you and I are not aligned on this.

I agree that correcting this behavior is necessary, but it must specifically be the responsibility of other men. Women have been attempting—unsuccessfully—for generations. From what I observe, many men still treat this behavior as acceptable or "not a big deal." Women cannot be expected to shoulder the burden of correcting it.

The implication that my perspective stems primarily from my experience with Seth really bothers me. I think I need to address that separately, because it opens a much larger conversation.

— — — — —

To: Laurel

From: Chris

Eventually, we're going to be in the same physical space. Writing will become outdated almost overnight. It's better that we adjust to having these kinds of conversations face-to-face. We just navigated a really difficult one successfully. I think it comes down to headspace—we're trying to solve problems, not win fights. That makes everything easier.

I apologize for my difficulty relating to the idea of women being responsible—or not responsible—for the actions of men. I'm not oblivious, and if I slow down and think about it, I can see your perspective. It's just not something that occupies my mental foreground. I tend to focus on what's within my immediate circle of influence. As a man, that circle is relatively small because we often direct our energy toward what's directly in front of us—specific tasks, specific people.

From what I observe, women tend to orient more toward relational dynamics and broader social patterns. That naturally makes you more attuned to systemic issues like this. When I step back and examine it that way, I can appreciate your position.

This does reflect a broader failure in our social fabric. The responsibility to correct behavior like that should fall on the people closest to him—his friends, his family. And yes, that includes the men in his life.

And while I don't intend to "blame" your experience for your perspective, I do think it significantly informs it. But I'll wait to hear your follow-up before drawing any conclusions.

— — — — —

To: Chris

From: Laurel

Thanks for taking the time to understand where I'm coming from. The problem I see, though, is this:

How many men actually sit down and think about this the way you just did? How many men have women in their lives who are able to articulate the depth of the problem the way I can? Do you realize how small a percentage you and I likely represent? We're basically unicorns. That's a frightening prospect for women who understand just how steep this uphill battle is.

And regarding men holding other men accountable—I honestly laughed at that assertion. Not because you're wrong (you absolutely ARE right), but because it rarely happens.

Look at how Joe's friends reacted when he walked out on his pregnant wife and special-needs son to move in with a woman ten years younger. Did any of them say a word? OF COURSE NOT. No one calls out bad behavior because it wouldn't be "supportive." I guarantee these same men see themselves as heroes in hypothetical scenarios that would require gallant defense of damsels in distress. Meanwhile, when confronted with a real-life situation demanding moral backbone, they look away rather than confront their friend for being the POS he is.

You'll see it again with the current fallout involving Steve when you return to social media. When I pointed out that he fell short of basic decency, I was labeled mean and spiteful. Men, by and large, do not tolerate criticism well— especially from women, even women they call friends. Instead of considering that I might be holding him to a higher standard because I know he's capable of it, the narrative became "Laurel is an asshole." Zero self-reflection. Zero accountability.

Anyway, I'm going to write the appendix regarding your suggestion that February is coloring these opinions. I honestly think that's the more important conversation for us right now.

Loves.

— — — — —

To: Laurel

From: Chris

This is, in part, a byproduct of PC culture. If there's even a chance that I (hypothetical me) could lose my job by putting my neck out to call someone out, I'm unlikely to do it. Replace "job" with "position in the social hierarchy," and you have a recipe for society's current dysfunction. People increasingly feel it's safer to stay out of the way of other people's metaphorical happiness than to risk social consequences for speaking plainly.

It only took a few generations of relative ease for this to become normalized. I think this dynamic also contributes to why many men, broadly speaking, are disengaging from civic and social life.

That said, I don't think we're as rare as you believe. I know a fair number of men in my field who think along similar lines—whether because of their upbringing (the Midwest tends to foster a certain practicality) or as a reaction against what they see as academic overreach. The cultural tide does shift, but it moves slowly. That's something people forget: societal change is glacial. Consider how long it takes a single person to meaningfully change their mind about something, and then multiply that by millions. There are occasional "hundredth-monkey" inflection points in history, but those are the exception, not the rule.

As for Steve—I saw that. What in the actual hell? Part of me hopes he recalibrates, but I'm not optimistic. He seems entrenched in ideology. There's no curiosity there, no willingness to engage another perspective. Often, it takes personal upheaval to disrupt that kind of rigidity, and I wouldn't wish that on him—or anyone.

I assume you're drafting one of your "Laurel Letters" right now to set the record straight.

Godspeed, love.

BLAMING FEBRUARY

To: Chris

From: Laurel

You still seem to think I'm hindered by February—that my opinions are clouded because of it. And maybe you're right. I don't think you are, but I'm not exactly the most objective person in this regard.

It frustrates me that you don't seem to trust that my logic is intact. Will you always assume I'm offended, disgruntled, wary, or frustrated because of Seth? That bothers me more than I can explain. It feels like I'll never be free of him—because even if I am, you'll still see me as tethered to him somehow.

Will you ever be able to see me without him lurking behind me?

And now I'm upset. Genuinely upset. Because if you can't, what chance do we have of making this work? I don't want to feel as if you're always looking past me at him.

Everything—from the "Cam Girl" conversation to what I'll now call "Creeper Dude"—has somehow circled back to February. You explicitly said I "ascribe a more negative point-of-view because of [my] experiences with Seth."

What am I supposed to do with that?

You routinely suggest—or flat out state—that I've arrived at my opinions because of February. That feels wildly unfair. It implies you don't believe I'm capable of logic untainted by trauma. How can we have equitable conversations if my thoughts, beliefs, and conclusions are consistently framed as broken ideology because I, myself, am broken?

I don't know what to do with this. I'm genuinely hurt.

I can accept that past experiences shape present perspectives. Of course they do. But it seems like the only experience that colors anything, in your mind, is February.

Can you not see me without seeing him?

Will I always just be some kind of broken trauma echo?

— — — — —

To: Laurel

From: Chris

"Hindered" isn't how I would put it.

As I said before, I think the event blew out your foundations, and you've had to rebuild them slowly. In that rebuilding, I think you've taken on more fault than you actually deserve. It's less a foundational failure and more an optimization problem.

And let me be clear: I don't think about him. I don't dwell on the event. I think about you—only you—and what might help you move through whatever issue is in front of you. I approach it the same way I would any other challenge you face. I want you free of unnecessary burden. Part of that is identifying what was actually within your locus of control. That still seems difficult for you at times, and you've acknowledged that yourself in prior emails about assuming responsibility even when something isn't your fault.

A good example is your marriage and divorce. You still beat yourself up for "choosing a terrible father for your children," but he lied to you in multiple ways. You made what you believed was the best decision based on false data. You had no reason to believe he was deceiving you. How is that your fault?

When Joe told you he didn't want children and didn't want to raise them with your values, you ended the engagement. You acted on the data presented. You only reconsidered when he changed the inputs—apologizing, expressing openness to children, agreeing to raise them with your moral framework. That's how rational decision-making works: you adjust based on new information. You had no reason to assume that information was false.

By the time you recognized the reality, you were already married and trying to salvage what you could because you're a good person and that's what good people do. He exploited your strength and goodwill until his behavior crossed a line that threatened your children. At that point, you made another decision based on the clearest data available.

That pattern is consistent. I don't doubt it will remain so.

If I've come down too hard regarding "blame," I apologize. This is complicated to articulate. The simplest way I can frame it is this: the assault was a catalyst that threw your internal order into chaos. The immediate problem is no longer the assault itself—it's the chaos that followed.

In a rough analogy, imagine someone breaking into your house and knocking everything off the shelves. Once the door is locked, the task becomes restoring order. Sometimes you even reorganize the shelves differently than before. You're in the middle of that reorganization, and yes, it began because someone came in and upended everything.

Are you more sensitive to certain topics because of your experience? Probably. That would be human. But do I believe your logic is broken or permanently tainted by trauma? Absolutely not. That's a leap I would never make.

You are painstakingly thoughtful. You juggle multiple perspectives effortlessly. You challenge your own assumptions for sport. Your insight into human behavior—and your ability to read people—is unsettlingly sharp.

If that respect hasn't been clear in our conversations, that's on me. I respect your mind as much as you respect mine.

What I worry about is not your intelligence—it's that you sometimes carry responsibility that isn't yours while you're still sorting through chaos that was never within your control. I want to be a grounding voice for you, not a diminishing one.

If my framing has felt dismissive or reductive, I'm sorry. But when I look at you, I see you. Him? He's not in the picture.

DIARY: ENTRY 22

——— ✕ ———

What a frustrating, vile mess I've found myself in. I've come to understand that when I flare this hot, this fast over something that appears trivial on the surface, the anger is usually a mask. So if I'm honest, I'm not furious. I'm hurt.

Steve posted something on social media. One of those posts—opinionated, emotionally charged, engineered to provoke agreement or outrage but very little nuance. I read it, thought a bit, then commented.

I knew my position wouldn't be popular, but it wasn't hateful. It wasn't racist, homophobic, or dismissive of anyone's humanity. I'm routinely accused of being too conservative by my left-leaning friends and too liberal by my right-leaning ones. Once again, I found myself squarely in that space.

Several friends had already engaged in the thread. Then one of Steve's friends—a man I do not know and who does not know me—responded. Not to the substance of the argument, and not even to the broader discussion, but directly to me. He called me names. He assigned motives and beliefs that were not mine. He painted me as something grotesque because it was easier than engaging with the logic I had presented.

At first, I brushed it off. I'm outspoken and articulate; ad hominem attacks are an expected fallback. I let it ride, assuming that any rebuttal would only reinforce his perception of me as some anonymous "hater" who deserved contempt for failing to toe the ideological line he'd drawn.

I waited. Not for agreement. Not for applause. Just for one person to say, "I know her. That's not who she is."

No one did.

Worse, when Steve responded—he AGREED with him.

Steve watched the exchange unfold. He knew the accusations were false. And still, when he spoke, he sided with his male friend because it was easier. Safer. Quieter.

That realization hurt more than the insults ever could. I felt profoundly alone.

I emailed them individually. I told them how deeply hurt I was—that when someone is maligned publicly, basic decency requires a response. Silence, in moments like that, is not neutral.

I reminded them that I have defended friends—publicly and privately—even when it was uncomfortable, because I believe integrity matters more than popularity.

Then I addressed the accusation itself.

I laid out the absurdity. I've dated a bisexual man. I've attended Pride rallies. I've fundraised for social justice organizations and continue to support those causes. Just days earlier, I had knelt on the pavement to wash the feet of a homeless gay man who had stepped on glass. Not for optics. Not for praise. Because he was hurting.

Full-on biblical nonsense. Knees on concrete. Ted's popcorn basin. Maria's flower vase as a pitcher.

And still, none of it mattered.

Because I questioned an all-or-nothing framework, I was recast as a bigot—and no one who claimed to know me felt compelled to correct it.

I told them this was the very double standard I had pointed out in the thread: both sides of the proverbial aisle claim moral superiority while often doing little to embody it.

Their inaction showed me how much they valued me—and it wasn't much.

I didn't send the message to burn bridges. I sent it because I believed—perhaps naively—that honesty might still salvage something.

SOCIAL MEDIA FALLOUT

To: Chris

From: Laurel

I know we already talked about it, but I ended up sending them one final message before granting myself closure. When I look back on this, I won't have regrets. They'll have understood me fully, and their response—or lack thereof—will be answer enough.

I wrestled with why I felt so angry about it, but after writing everything out, I realized it wasn't anger as much as hurt. And given everything else I'm juggling, this felt like an especially cruel ball to throw my way.

Such is life, I suppose. It has a way of revealing who people really are. I should probably be grateful to have learned it now rather than in a moment when it truly counted.

I imagine they're all licking their wounds right now—and deservedly so. They acted like cowards and assumed you'd be your typical gracious self and let it roll.

Everyone knows you can handle yourself. Because they know you'll defend yourself, they feel no responsibility to step in on your behalf in situations like that. What's especially twisted is that they've all benefited from your willingness to fight for fairness and integrity, yet saw no need to get their hands dirty for you.

Didn't you go to bat for Patrice against Aaron over her wedding? Didn't you challenge the entire friend group when Steve was hesitant about getting serious with Kiera? Haven't they all, at one point or another, come to you for help navigating something because they were either too intimidated or too ill-equipped to do it themselves?

Let them sit with it. You didn't deserve to have your name dragged because some insecure idiot felt threatened by reality. You deserved friends who would publicly defend who you are—especially when they know the truth.

Their silence says more about them than it ever will about you.

DIARY: ENTRY 23

———✕———

I thought I could compartmentalize the Steve situation the way I've compartmentalized everything else. One wound here, another there. Tidy. Manageable.

Pfft. Fat chance, Laurel. Fat chance.

What happened in that thread lodged itself in the very place I've been trying so desperately to rebuild: my willingness to trust people with the truth of what happened to me.

Honestly, I didn't mind letting go of the other two. But Steve? He had always struck me as someone willing to go the distance when it came to injustice. After my separation from Joe, he was one of the few mutual friends who made a point of assuring me I hadn't been iced out. He even asked my permission before inviting Joe's girlfriend to his apartment in New York.

I trusted Steve. I trusted his wife, Kiera.

When things first began unraveling, I intentionally reached out to Kiera because of her background in trauma counseling. I gave her permission to share my story with Steve—though I don't believe she ever did. Not that it ultimately matters. I wouldn't have wanted his knowledge of it to shape how he treated me. Still... I expected better. This behavior? I could brace for it from Patrice, certainly from Gene—but from Steve? The disappointment is profound.

I was already walking a narrow bridge. Every day felt like a negotiation between speaking and staying silent, honesty and self-protection. I was trying to convince myself that telling the truth wouldn't cost me everything. That people could know—and still see me. Not a victim. Not a cautionary tale. Just me.

How could I trust them with February—something soaked in stigma, shame, and social landmines—when they couldn't manage a single sentence in my defense over a social media disagreement?

That realization pulled the rug out from under me.

I felt myself retreat. I stopped considering who might be safe to tell. I stopped imagining conversations that might lead to healing. I began folding inward again—carefully, deliberately—undoing progress I had fought hard to make.

What makes it worse is how confidently they speak about injustice. They post. They comment. They know the language. They brand themselves allies, advocates—the "good ones."

They are loud when injustice is abstract and costs nothing. But when it's real—messy, uncomfortable, implicating someone they know—their voices evaporate.

It's the same pattern I saw during my divorce from Joe, when I learned he had been cheating. People didn't want to get involved. They didn't want to "choose sides." No one wanted to call him out for abandoning his pregnant wife and special-needs son to chase Peter Pan from dusk till dawn.

It isn't that they fail to recognize injustice. They simply don't want to pay the price of opposing it.

Everyone is a keyboard warrior. No one wants to be a real-life crossing guard.

Standing up for me online would have required confronting a man Steve considers a friend. Speaking up would disrupt social equilibrium. Steve sees that man regularly. I'm tucked two states away. Why risk tension? Why endure the discomfort of being perceived as ideologically aligned with "the enemy"?

And then I think about how often rape victims are told to speak up. To tell someone. To trust the process. To believe we'll be supported.

Who, exactly, is supposed to make that safe?

There is nothing about this that feels safe. And "trust the process"? Please. The process is designed to consume survivors.

THIS is why women stay quiet. Not because we are weak—because we are observant.

We watch how people handle small truths before we hand them the big ones.

And when the people who claim to care about you choose silence—choose ease, choose themselves—it teaches you to guard your voice.

Right now, the hardest part of healing isn't the memory of what was done to me; it's learning whom I can trust not to look away.

RE: SOCIAL MEDIA FALLOUT

———✕———

To: Chris

From: Laurel

Ha ha, you are seriously the best, love. Having your fiery support more than makes up for this. Really... my heart genuinely feels better having read your tirade. If nothing else, I know I have you in my corner, and honestly, that's more than enough for me. I love you.

— — — — —

To: Laurel

From: Chris

What are you going to do about Kiera? She knows about everything. Has she even reached out to check on you? Did she ever tell Steve? In brighter news, we'll be together soon in Colorado. I can't wait to wrap you in my arms. And bedsheets.

DIARY: ENTRY 24

———✕———

I almost blacked out on Colorado—and Jenn's wedding.

I mean, I knew it was coming. I knew I needed to book an Airbnb and figure out flights and logistics, but oh my gosh, it's right around the corner and I have nothing in order. I don't even know if I still fit into the bridesmaid dress. And shoot—did I order the sneakers for the reception? Dear God, I'm a mess. I still need to put together a proper blessing since she was kind enough to ask me.

Gah. I guess I'm really in this now.

I've been going back and forth for months about dropping out. Beyond the constant exhaustion and stress, I'm terrified of actually attending this wedding. Jenn is in the Air Force, and she's marrying another Air Force member. There will probably be a hundred uniforms there, and I keep having these ridiculous visions of their somehow figuring out I'm the one who "ratted out" their friend. The one who lied about rape and assault. The one who tried to ruin their charming, funny Seth for attention.

In these visions—because what else do I call them?—they're all connected to him, and I'm automatically the villain. No one needs my side of the story because they don't need it. They're friends with him, just as Krista was, so of course he must be telling the truth. He can't possibly be the problem. It has to be me. And my mere presence somehow taints Jenn's wedding.

Obviously, this is completely far-fetched. I know that. Not every Air Force member knows every other Air Force member. These people are stationed half a country away. No one knows who I am. And even if, by some microscopic chance, someone did know Seth, the odds of their connecting me to him are even smaller.

But logic and emotion rarely occupy the same lane.

Sigh.

Understanding rationally that this isn't a big deal does nothing to calm my nerves. When I think about this trip, I feel actual panic. I hate that. I am genuinely thrilled for Jenn and her daughter, Lisa. I'm so happy they've found a good man who loves them both deeply. I love this for them. I even love it for Tim.

But I'd be lying if I said this whole thing doesn't terrify me— because it does. It's irrational, yes. But truth is truth.

Regardless, I'm going. I'm going to show up. I'm going to celebrate. I refuse to let fear dictate my movements.

And I get to see Natasha! It's been forever. I'll finally meet her husband and kids, and I cannot wait. Silver linings abound.

And of course, I'll get to see Chris. That alone steadies me. He'll be there through the wedding, which means it will be fine... right?

Famous last words, perhaps. But I'm choosing to believe this will be good.

It will be good. I will be good.

COLORADO

To: Chris

From: Laurel

I booked us an adorable Airbnb! It's so cute and super close to the venue. There are little shops all along the main drag and even a breakfast spot nearby. I also confirmed plans with Natasha—I cannot WAIT for you to meet her. She's wonderful, and her kids are adorable. I'm really looking forward to meeting her husband. I feel as if I already know him from all the pictures and posts she's shared over the years. Isn't it strange how social media has completely reshaped the way we get to know people? Wild.

As for the wedding, I appreciated our conversation last night. I know my fears are far-fetched, but I'm grateful you didn't treat them as if they were ridiculous. I talked with Jenn and Clare (the maid of honor) about the rehearsal dinner and day-of logistics—makeup, hair, all of it. I think we're squared away. It's going to be so good to see Jenn and Lisa. I'm choosing to focus on that and trust that everything else will sort itself out.

By the way, I can't remember if I told you, but the bridesmaid dresses are red. Very pretty, honestly. Do with that information what you will.

Just a couple more weeks and we'll be together again. My body misses yours.

— — — — —

To: Laurel

From: Chris

Mine misses yours too, love. Work's been brutal lately, so this will be a welcome break. The weather can be dicey this time of year, but we've always managed to get lucky.

I'm sure you booked a perfect place—you always do.

And your fears aren't insane. I do think your logical brain is right to label them far-fetched, but they're not irrational. I'll be there the entire time. You'll see your friends, and I'll keep you dancing. Whatever happens, we'll face it together. Though if a red dress is involved, I can certainly make a few guesses as to what will be happening. Loves.

WEDDING RECAP

To: Jenn

From: Laurel

Okay, I apologize in advance for sounding like a total asshole at the beginning of this, but I promise it makes sense by the end. Here goes...

I was TERRIFIED of your wedding. I cannot even begin to tell you how many times I wanted to bow out completely. Mind you, I was THRILLED for you and Tom. I was so happy you were starting your lives together, and that he's so wonderful with Lisa. You know I'll take any excuse to see you. But your wedding scared the absolute shit out of me.

Why?

Air Force. That's why.

Also, your Air Force buddy Todd was actually a really nice guy. So that was helpful.

Even though I know the odds of your having any connection to Seth are basically zero, the idea of being surrounded by a bunch of Air Force members sent me into a tailspin. But I sucked it up because f*ck it—I love you, and being there mattered more than my fear.

Fast forward to the rehearsal luncheon. It was lovely... and then you paired me with Todd. Again, I recognize my own irrationality here, so please don't feel bad, but it scared me more than I expected. I tried really hard to mask it, and I'm sorry I failed at that. That's why I bowed out early. I still feel awful about leaving, and I'm truly sorry.

I peppered Clare with questions: Would there be a lot of Air Force people? Would anyone be in dress uniform? Did she know which guests were Air Force? (That's how I found out about Todd.) I'm sure she thought I was insane. Maybe she already knew I was. Who knows? The point is, I spiraled myself into a frenzy.

Chris picked me up, and the second I got into the car, I dissolved. Tears. Full meltdown. Not my finest moment.

The next morning was worse. Shaking. Crying. Anxiety through the roof. And Chris wasn't going to be around until the wedding itself. Perfect. But I was determined not to ruin anything. So I put on my game face. Again, if I seemed off, please know that was about me—not you.

Everything was going smoothly until right before the ceremony, when Chris texted that he had forgotten his shirt. HOW do you forget your shirt when flying out for a wedding? I don't know. But my rocket scientist of a man somehow managed it.

That meant he'd miss the ceremony—and might miss the reception, too. The very reception I'd been low-grade panicking about attending alone.

When I got that text, I actually laughed and said (to God), "Oh. So You really want me to do this by myself?"

He sure did!

It felt like being shoved out of the nest and told to either fly or crash. I flew. Nothing bad happened. Everything was not just okay—it was beautiful. And Chris managed to buy a shirt and meet me at the reception anyway.

But by then, it didn't matter. I had done it alone.

Jenn, I had been having daily nightmares. DAILY. I basically haven't slept in a year. But after making it through your wedding, something shifted. It felt as if I'd crossed some invisible barrier I didn't even know existed. Things have been SO MUCH BETTER since then.

I needed you to know that. Beyond loving you all to pieces, I now carry this immense gratitude for that day. So… there's my wedding word-vomit.

— — — — —

To: Laurel

From: Jenn

Oh my gosh. I am so, so sorry it never occurred to me that pairing you with Todd could have been a trigger. I feel awful. I knew it would be a stressful time for you, but that particular detail just didn't cross my mind, and I'm really sorry.

That said—I am so glad this ended up helping you.

You are not crazy. None of this sounds crazy. It makes total sense, and you don't need to beat yourself up for feeling scared or overwhelmed. What was wrong was what that piece of shit did to you—not how you reacted afterward.

But we're not giving him airtime. We're focusing on your healing, sleeping, thriving. I am so proud of you.

You are an absolute force, and I'm so grateful you're in my life.

I truly hope you and Chris had a wonderful time. And again, I'm sorry if anything added to your stress—but I'm so, so happy you're doing better.

So… sorry/not sorry for being part of your breakthrough?

It's like, "Thanks, God—but maybe You owe us a stiff drink." Ha!

Love you. Now convince Chris to move to Colorado so we can be neighbors.

— — — — —

To: Jenn

From: Laurel

Ha! Colorado is actually on our short list. We LOVED it out there. It's stunning. Having you as a neighbor would just be the cherry on top.

And please—do not feel guilty about any of this. You were orchestrating an epic wedding. I should have been the last thing on your mind. I don't feel slighted in the slightest. I love you stupid amounts and am so grateful I got to stand with you.

But yes, God definitely owes us a round of stiff drinks.

Love you, toooooo!

COLORADO CATCH UP

To: Chris

From: Laurel

I did write two more pages in the journal over the last couple of days—mostly out of spite, if I'm honest. I wanted to prove that I *could* write in it. And I did. Two pages. I've got three left now. Whatever. The point is, I wrote. I'm slowly resigning myself to the fact that I'll probably need another book.

I listened to a podcast late last night that really resonated. It talked about the need for time and space to process things. I don't talk to my family about this. I don't talk to friends. I try not to burden you with it too much.

So that leaves me with my stupid little book—and I hadn't even been allowing myself to use that.

How am I supposed to process any of this fully if I keep restricting my outlets?

I think this circles back to your point about therapy. You want me to be forced to process because you know I'm not really processing with anyone else. (At least that was my 3 a.m. realization while mentally replaying our conversation for the thousandth time.)

So that's where I'm at. I'm okay—just tired. Really, really tired. But also feeling good, because I know real progress was made this weekend. It's just a lot while juggling the boys, the new house, and work.

Whew. Really looking forward to seeing you again.

— — — — —

To: Laurel

From: Chris

I empathize. When I'm stressed, I default to over-analysis, so I've walked that road myself. I'm glad you see where I was coming from. Like I said, I needed time to think it through. I don't like reacting impulsively, but I also needed to be honest about where my head was in that moment.

Note to self: spite is a powerful motivator.

In all seriousness, I'm really glad you went back to journaling.

In situations like this, not talking through your processes can create a negative feedback loop. I still believe you may just need a better therapeutic fit.

We clearly have different definitions of "okay." That's been the main source of my frustration. But as with everything else, I'm confident we'll sort it out.

You're doing incredible work, love. I'm proud of you. Truly. You're a masterclass in internal strength.

Also, I'm having a very difficult time not picturing you in that dress. Let's get that back into rotation. Fuck.

— — — — —

To: Chris

From: Laurel

That makes sense, and I appreciate that you were simply expressing where you were mentally. In the future, I think I'll be far less defensive if you explicitly say that's what you're doing. It should be obvious, but in the heat of things, my instincts default to combat mode—assuming you're punishing me or signaling disappointment.

I recognize that's my baggage. I just don't recognize it in the moment. After I've had time to mull things over, I usually see where I overcorrected. So yes—if you say, "I'm just telling you where my head is," that will probably help me diffuse my own nonsense. I *know* you're not trying to hurt me.

This weekend changed something.

I knew it would. I just didn't realize how drastically. I thought I'd feel relieved afterward. I thought I'd sleep better. I assumed I'd cling to you the entire time. I was honestly afraid I'd have another rehearsal-brunch moment where I'd ask you to take me home.

Even knowing it was 99.9% in my head, it terrified me. And it's embarrassing to admit that. How do you fear something you logically know isn't real?

But you let me have my moment. Thank you for that. Thank you for not calling me ridiculous—even if you might have thought it. Getting it out beforehand helped tremendously. I vented, and then I was able to set it aside and focus on giving Jenn the best day possible. And I think she had it.

I think I needed to prove to myself that I could do that. Maybe that's why God let you forget your shirt. It felt like being shoved out of the nest—but necessary.

And as usual, He was right.

I needed to face the fear without using you as a safety net. I did. And I feel really, *really* good about that. I even went out of my way to be warm toward Todd just to prove to myself that I could.

I'm not afraid anymore.

It feels as if I got my edge back. I've been cowering for so long, and this weekend forced me out of the corner. I'm proud of that. It might sound silly—being proud of conquering a fear that technically never materialized—but it feels as if I crossed a threshold.

I feel lighter. Stronger. Freer.

I'm still exhausted, but something tells me I'm finally going to start sleeping again. And that makes me almost giddy.

Thank you for coming. This would not have happened without you. You made it possible, and I need you to understand how deeply I appreciate that.

I didn't expect Colorado to be as therapeutic as it was. I don't feel "fixed"—not entirely—but I don't feel broken and teetering anymore. The pieces I've been rebuilding finally feel stable.

When I asked you about your definition of "okay" in Colorado, I was frustrated. Your version made sense—and yes, it's probably more accurate than mine—but it inevitably led us back to therapy.

I'll admit something: I was annoyed when you told me you'd never actually gone to a therapist yourself and that it was your GP who prescribed things. Not because you came to respect the profession later—but because it felt hypocritical to push me toward something you hadn't done.

I slept on that. And I realized that growth changes perspective. You evolved. So why was I irritated that you were trying to use what you'd learned to help me?

Again, my default seems to be angry defensiveness. But give me a few hours, and I generally find my way back to clarity.

Mmmm. I love you, too. And if you want that dress in rotation, I'll happily wear it when you pick me up from the airport.

Muahz.

— — — — —

To: Laurel

From: Chris

I think you're over-rationalizing a bit and giving yourself more grief than you deserve. There *are* things to fear in this world. The challenge is learning to differentiate between actual danger and situations where you're objectively safe.

When you're in a room full of people, the odds of something strange happening are near zero—but not technically zero. Some random guy *could* run in and do something horrific. But 99.9% of the time, that's not going to happen. The key is calibrating appropriately, not eliminating caution altogether.

As for the journal, it might actually be cathartic to close it out intentionally. If the wedding really marked the shift you're describing, documenting that transition could be meaningful.

I'll almost always give you the space to get what you need out, babe. I've said it before, but I genuinely believe discussion is where the magic happens. You have to build the thought, shape it, and articulate it clearly enough that the other person can truly understand what you're trying to convey. That process matters.

And regarding the rehearsal—I still feel bad about leaving you to handle it on your own. But I'm genuinely thrilled it turned out the way it did.

I think you're slightly underplaying the usefulness of fear and slightly overplaying your reaction to it. Being observant and cautious is healthy. Overconfidence isn't. But beyond that, I'm incredibly happy that you feel lighter. I could absolutely tell during the wedding. You were moving like someone unburdened. It was amazing to watch.

And of course, you're welcome. I had a fantastic time. And yes—I know how much you appreciate me. I'm grateful for that.

Regarding therapy: during our conversation, I realized I hadn't been as clear as I should have been. I've written before about dismissing the therapist I saw in college—only to later recognize that he was largely correct. Therapists are human and imperfect, but they serve an important role—much like Judeo-Christian values in society. I've simply been fortunate not to require sustained therapy myself.

That said, I still think it's worth another drive-by for you. A better fit might make all the difference.

Soon, love. Soon. I'll be waiting for you in that dress.

DIARY: ENTRY 25

———✕———

Y a know, there is a version of this story in which the assault is the defining event. There is another in which Chris is. Neither is true.

February didn't define me, and I sure as hell won't let it define my future. What it did was force me to recalibrate my threshold for "nice" and my understanding of strength.

I had mistaken politeness for intuition. I labeled fear as logic. Worst of all, what I once called strength was really endurance. Recalibration became my obsession.

I told myself this was wisdom.

Oh, Laurel... it wasn't wisdom; it was over-correction.

My instincts worked; I simply overrode them in the name of civility. That wasn't a flaw of character—it was conditioning. Women are trained to treat politeness as morality and self-abandonment as survival.

I paid for that distinction with February and all its aftermath.

For months, I conflated vigilance with virtue. If I could anticipate every male movement, pre-sort humanity into competent or malevolent, align myself with the largest protector in the room, I would be safe; but safety built on constant assessment isn't safety; it's occupation.

And I refuse to live as occupied territory.

Chris didn't swoop in with a cape, but he stood steady. He became the lighthouse my chaos could crash against. He allowed space for the competing tensions—desire and shame, hope and fear. He helped me name the threads of chaos, but I was the one who did the work of unraveling them one knot at a time.

My body remembers what my mind tried to intellectualize. But it also relearns.

It relearns that intimacy can be chosen, that "no" can be honored, and that fear can surge—and recede. I no longer need to burn the bed, and I no longer need to prove I am "okay."

When something feels wrong, I don't negotiate with it or soften it into humor. I certainly do not invite it inside. And when something feels right—steady, grounded, reciprocal—I don't punish it for what came before.

I still carry February. It surfaces in conversations, in research rabbit holes, in the reflex to scan a room. But it no longer dictates the architecture of my relationships—or my future.

I inhabit my body again.

I WIN, AND THAT'S THAT

To: Chris

From: Laurel

I think the subject line says it all, babe: I don't need the therapist.

I no longer feel the need for someone else to validate what I already know. I no longer confuse vigilance with wisdom. A terrible thing happened. It rattled foundational pieces within me. But I am capable of rebuilding those foundations in a way that ultimately benefits me. I refuse to let this define me or dictate my future.

I accept that it will be a lens through which I see the world. But that isn't inherently tragic.

Galileo could see the stars because he learned how to stack lenses in a way that brought clarity. This is simply another lens in my arsenal. Motherhood is one. Betrayal is one. What happened with Steve. With Joe. With Mary and Theresa and Sunny and Michel and Xavier and you and Jenn and Natasha and Cat. Every person, every fracture, every grace—each adds dimension. The heavens don't disappear because the glass changes; they come into sharper focus.

As long as I remain committed to honest self-reflection and disciplined awareness, I will be OK. And yes, I'm using my definition—even if yours is fancier.

Mine fits me.

OK is not the absence of pain; it is the presence of agency. It is waking up without requiring consensus in order to trust my own perception. It is understanding that what happened altered my architecture but did not collapse it. I carry more lenses now—motherhood, betrayal, violence, love—but none of them get to dominate the view.

OK is allowing people to fail me without restructuring myself to compensate for their cowardice. It is recognizing that trust is no longer default—it is earned, deliberate, reciprocal. It is living without confusing endurance with virtue, without outsourcing belief, and without demanding closure, forgiveness, or applause.

I see more now. I carry more now. And I am more discerning about who walks beside me.

As for you? You have a standing invitation.

I can't promise anything fancier than that red dress, but I can promise you're welcome to take me out of it anytime your little heart desires. I'm yours—in all my chaotic, fully "OK" glory.

But only because I am mine first. Wholly. Unapologetically. Without pretense.

Thank you for helping me find myself again.

Loves.

AFTERWORD

The last email in this book was not the end of the story. It was simply the end of the part that needed to be written while it was still raw.

I did not write this book to offer a model of recovery; this is not a guide.

These pages were never meant to become a narrative. They were a means of survival, written to hold what I could not carry alone, without the obligation of coherence or resolution. When I began shaping them into a book, I worried that imposing structure might distort the truth. Trauma does not arrive or depart neatly, and healing does not follow a timetable that makes for satisfying conclusions.

What ultimately convinced me to finish *Laurel's Diary* was the realization that silence is also a kind of shaping—and one that rarely favors those who have been harmed.

This book does not extract meaning from violence. Rape is not a blessing in disguise; it is violence. What it documents instead is the quieter aftermath: the way trauma alters one's internal architecture without necessarily destroying it; the way trust, intimacy, and self-perception must be renegotiated rather than restored.

For a long time, I had resisted the language of "being okay." It felt reductive, even dishonest. But over time, I came to understand that *okay* does not mean the absence of pain; it means the presence of agency. It means waking up without needing the world to agree with me in order to trust my own perception. It means recognizing that what happened to me changed the way I see—but did not collapse my ability to see.

I carry more lenses now. Motherhood. Betrayal. Violence. Love. None of them must become the only way I understand the world. Learning to live has meant choosing which lenses I rely on, and when. It has meant allowing people to fail me without reorganizing myself to compensate for their cowardice. It has meant understanding that trust is no longer a default setting, but a deliberate, earned exchange.

Some readers may wish for more distance, more reflection, more certainty. I understand that impulse. Distance can feel safer. But I chose to preserve much of this language as it was written because it is the most accurate record I have—not of what happened, but of how it lived inside me afterward. The repetition, the circular thinking, the moments of clarity followed by collapse: these were not editorial oversights. They were lived experiences.

I am no longer the woman who wrote many of these pages. I am also not wholly free of what shaped them. Both things are true. Living with that paradox has become part of my life, and telling this story has been part of learning how to hold it—without performance, without apology, and without requiring closure.

For those who recognize themselves here: you are not alone, and you do not owe anyone a version of your survival that feels tidy or inspiring. Endurance is not virtue. Healing is not a spectacle. And "okay," when defined on your own terms, is enough.